Shakespeare and Lecoq

ARDEN PERFORMANCE COMPANIONS

Series Editors: Michael Dobson, Abigail Rokison-Woodall and Simon
Russell Beale

Published titles

Shakespearean Rhetoric by Benet Brandreth
'You' and 'Thou' in Shakespeare by Penelope Freedman
Shakespeare and Meisner by Aileen Gonsalves and Tracy Irish

Further titles in preparation

Shakespeare and Stanislavsky by Annie Tyson
Shakespeare and Laban by Jacquelyn Bessell and Laura Weston
Shakespeare and Brecht by Stephen Unwin

Arden Performance Editions

Series Editors: Michael Dobson, Abigail Rokison-Woodall and Simon
Russell Beale

Published titles

A Midsummer Night's Dream edited by Abigail Rokison-Woodall
As You Like It edited by Nora Williams
Hamlet edited by Abigail Rokison-Woodall
King Lear edited by Simon Russell Beale and Abigail Rokison-
Woodall
Macbeth edited by Katherine Brokaw
Much Ado About Nothing edited by Anna Kamaralli
Othello edited by Paul Prescott
Romeo and Juliet edited by Abigail Rokison-Woodall
The Tempest edited by Miranda Fay Thomas
Twelfth Night edited by Gretchen Minton

Further titles in preparation

The Winter's Tale edited by Robert Shaughnessy
Richard III edited by Abigail Rokison-Woodall and
Simon Russell Beale

Shakespeare and Lecoq

A Practical Guide for Actors, Directors, Students and Teachers

Ed Woodall and Abigail Rokison-Woodall

THE ARDEN SHAKESPEARE
LONDON · NEW YORK · OXFORD · NEW DELHI · SYDNEY

THE ARDEN SHAKESPEARE
Bloomsbury Publishing Plc
50 Bedford Square, London, WC1B 3DP, UK
1385 Broadway, New York, NY 10018, USA
29 Earlsfort Terrace, Dublin 2, Ireland

BLOOMSBURY, THE ARDEN SHAKESPEARE and the Arden Shakespeare logo
are trademarks of Bloomsbury Publishing Plc

First published in Great Britain 2024

Series design by Charlotte Daniels
Cover image © Igor Stevanovic / Alamy

A catalogue record for this book is available from the British Library.

A catalog record for this book is available from the Library of Congress.

ISBN: HB: 978-1-3502-4408-5
PB: 978-1-3502-4409-2
ePDF: 978-1-3502-4410-8
eBook: 978-1-3502-4411-5

Series: Arden Performance Companions

Typeset by Deanta Global Publishing Services, Chennai, India
Printed and bound in Great Britain

To find out more about our authors and books visit www.bloomsbury.com
and sign up for our newsletters.

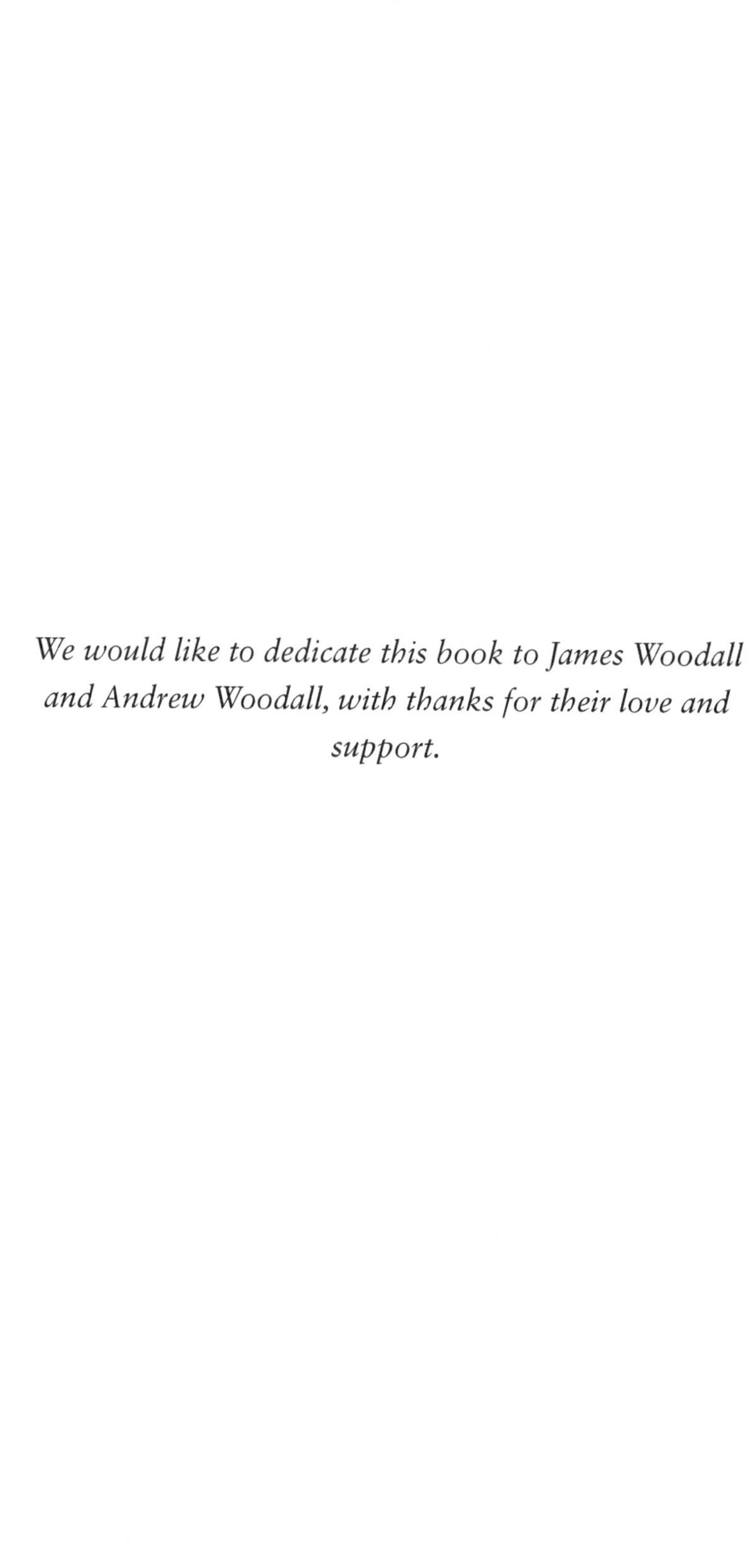

We would like to dedicate this book to James Woodall and Andrew Woodall, with thanks for their love and support.

CONTENTS

LIST OF VIDEOS

We have created videos as practical examples for various exercises in this book. To watch them please visit https://bloomsbury.pub/shakespeare-and-lecoq

Films made by Anthony Greyley of OX Productions
Films feature: Molly Keogh, Ed Woodall and Abigail Rokison-Woodall

SERIES PREFACE

The Arden Performance Companions offers practice-focused introductions to different aspects of staging Shakespeare's plays: whether accounts of how Shakespearean drama may respond to particular systems of rehearsal and preparation, guides to how today's actors can understand and use different facets of Shakespeare's verbal style or explorations of how particular modern practitioners have used Shakespeare's scripts as starting points for their own embodied thinking about the social and aesthetic possibilities of popular theatre.

The premise of this series is that the interpretation of Shakespeare not only is confined to the literary analysis of his scripts but also includes their rehearsal and performance. With this in mind, the Arden list of editions of Shakespeare expanded in 2017 to include not only heavily annotated scholarly texts of each play, designed primarily for use in colleges and universities, but a new series, the Arden Performance Editions of Shakespeare, designed primarily for use in rehearsal rooms and at drama schools. Just as academic editions of Shakespeare may be supplemented by books introducing students to different modes of academic criticism, so these Arden Performance Companions seek to supplement the Arden Performance Editions, offering a rich variety of practical guidance on how Shakespeare's plays can be brought to life in contemporary performance.

Note on texts

All extracts from the Shakespearean text are taken from the Arden 3 texts, accessed through Drama Online.

AUTHOR'S PREFACE
Ed Woodall

A few years ago, Abigail suggested to me that I come and teach a Lecoq workshop at the Shakespeare Institute in Stratford-upon-Avon. She had been introduced to Lecoq's work via the inspirational movement teacher Christian Darley, at LAMDA, where she trained as an actor and now as a Shakespearean academic was used to teaching practical Shakespeare modules based on the work of various theatre practitioners, including Lecoq. It dawned on her that her newish brother-in-law had trained with Lecoq and had been teaching the work for nearly thirty years, intensively at the Oxford School of Drama for the last ten years, and that it would be great for the students to experience the work directly from a Lecoq-trained practitioner. I took up the offer and went, once a year, to give a Lecoq-meets-Shakespeare workshop at the Institute. The workshops involved getting students to play, consider space and be taught seemingly abstract movements, before segueing into exploring Shakespeare characters and speeches. As a three-hour workshop it was always fun and successful. In one session, Abi came to watch. I was confident of the work but, as ever, when your boss comes to check in on you, I felt some trepidation. I got about half an hour in and Abi, who was seated at a desk on the side of the room, beckoned me over, and whispered, 'This is great! You should write a book on it.' I was understandably buoyed by this, but writing a book felt like too big an undertaking; I had already floundered with a book on my own Lecoq-inspired acting technique for this publisher and was not sure I had it in me. The idea drifted away until Abi came back to me in 2020 with a proposition that we co-write a book on Shakespeare and Lecoq. It was the year of the pandemic and I was actually in the midst of a career shift into teaching Feldenkrais Method online and was not sure I had the time, and so I settled down to write an email excusing myself one

Sunday afternoon in June. As I was making my excuses, something, the spirit of both Shakespeare and Lecoq maybe, came over me, and I started to explore an exercise around Lecoq's seven levels of tension and Orsino's opening speech in *Twelfth Night*. I was still at it two hours later, having had a whale of a time, and by that stage, I had changed my mind. If this exercise is so good, I thought, then there must be more to be explored! I wrote the rest of a proposal and before too long we had been commissioned to write the book. There have, of course, been twists and turns and ups and downs as we have collaborated on this book but Abi has been to my acting workshops and I have learned the basic tenets of academic writing and more than that, we have formed a great team. It has been a pure joy to collaborate with such a professional, compassionate and clever person. I know she must have been pulling her hair out occasionally as I stumbled around the subject and struggled to understand the perspective of the book and the notion of a deadline, but in the end, we have put something together of which we are both really proud. It has been a journey of great learning for both of us and we trust that our book will be a journey of great learning for you too.

Postscript by Abigail Rokison-Woodall

Ed has given an excellent account of the origins of this book, so I will add only a postscript. When I suggested that we set out to collaborate on this book, my knowledge of Lecoq was fairly rudimentary. I had used some of his exercises, passed down to me through drama school and directors with whom I had worked, in my module on Shakespeare and Theatre Practice at the Shakespeare Institute (before I invited Ed to contribute to this) but had always found *The Moving Body* rather obscure and quite difficult to work from. I did know, however, that Lecoq needed to feature in our Arden Shakespeare Performance Companions series, alongside other key practitioners whose work has been central to Western acting practice and training. I knew that his work could be very helpful for creating character and for story-telling, but, until co-authoring this book, I hadn't appreciated the many synergies between the work of Shakespeare and Lecoq, particularly in terms of their shared vocabulary of imagery and metaphor – colours, elements, animals, materials. In the process of putting the book together, I have learnt a great deal from Ed about the work of Lecoq. Ed has been a brilliant, generous, creative collaborator and has helped me to understand better some of Lecoq's key ideas and practices. I hope that this book helps you to better understand them as well.

FOREWORD – 'ARE WE ALLOWED TO SPEAK?' BY TOBY JONES

There are thirty of us sitting on the sprung, wooden floor of the converted boxing arena in which Lecoq ran his school. It is late on a Friday afternoon, the end of the week and as usual we're tired, excited and confused. Most of us have questions about the task, the auto-cours, we've just been set. 'Auto-cours' is the short performance students devise in response to the techniques and themes we learn in class.

'Can we use words?'
Versions of this question surface every week and Lecoq
   invariably responds,
'Of course you can use words. If you need them.'

I'm often asked if I went to mime school. 'No', I respond, somewhat defensively. I suppose we did learn some mime but Lecoq (the school has become synonymous with the man) wasn't a mime school. It still isn't. Writing is at the core of the school but it is often approached through silence. Rather than reading and re-reading a text to discover the motivations and impulses that may have inspired it, students at Lecoq are encouraged to discover the function of a piece of text by exploring the silence that preceded and necessitated it. What has made these words inevitable? How do words complement, colour and counterpoint the physical expression of the body and the space in which that body is moving? How do we make the text dynamic? What prompted these words? Why was the silence broken?

In the following chapters much of what Lecoq described as 'the voyage through the school' is mapped out in the service of Shakespeare's plays. Although no plays, not even Shakespeare, are taught at the school, the skills, spirit and ethos of its pedagogy are rooted in the classical and early modern European theatre. It is an international school that encourages its students to learn through inherited techniques, practical observation, experiment and play.

Lecoq furnished his students with an abundant supply of resources with which to replay and perform the world around us. And then to understand how a text might further reveal that world. He encouraged us to retrieve our concrete experiences of the rhythms, elements, materials and colour in the manifest world in order to arrive at the abstraction and transposition of the written word or the play.

This book evokes the restless, hilarious, frustrating and revelatory experience of the school. Step by step Ed and Abigail adapt these exercises and experiments to invite the actor into the uniquely rich and complex dramatic poetry of Shakespeare's plays. Their connections, suggestions and propositions will help practitioners to broaden their study of Shakespeare's plays intuitively and kinetically.

Two paradoxes . . . If this book requires the actors to leave the table and move in the rehearsal space, they will often return to that table with a better understanding of stillness. And the textures of Shakespeare's rhetoric, verse and imagery will be reinvigorated by the exploration of sound, story and yes . . . silence.

ACKNOWLEDGEMENTS

Apart from the collaboration between the authors, this book is the result of many other collaborations with actors, academics, students and directors. First, we would like to thank those who have been interviewed in preparation of the book: Emily Ernst from Fair Assembly, Emma Rice, Tom Morris, Rick Katz, Scott Handy, Elliott Shrimpton, Annabel Arden, Carolina Valdés, Darren Tunstall, Toby Jones, John Wright, Jonathan Becker, Simon McBurney, Ayse Tashkiran, Sabina Netherclift, Briony O'Callaghan, Jane Gibson, Henry Maynard, Sara Romersberger, Phyllida Lloyd, Linus Tundström, Tom Dixon, Barbara Houseman, Sasha Plaige, Olly Crick, Catherine Alexander, Aurelian Koch, GH Zonana, Amy Russell and the inimitable Paddy Hayter from Footsbarn.

Thanks must go to our colleagues: Ed's colleagues at Oxford School of Drama – George Peck for his inspirational work on Shakespeare, Kirsty McFarland for showing the way with movement, Steve Woodward and the voice team of Joanna Weir Ouston, Ben Joiner and Ashley Howard; and Abigail's colleagues at the Shakespeare Institute and to all the students at OSD and the Shakespeare Institute, in particular Louis Simon, Kaitlyn Stine, Ben Simon, Steve Rogers, Lisa Vanco, Rhiannon McDonagh and Jack Butler, who have helped directly with exercises in the book. Thank you to Micaela Miranda for inviting Ed to teach work related to this book on recent Shakespeare Summer Schools. Thanks to the actors who came to Shakespeare and Lecoq workshops: Georgina Fairbanks, Emily Largier, Joey Holden, Peter Kenny (for his acting and his generosity), Geoff Beale, Caroline O'Mahoney, Duncan Taylor, John Alderman, Rebecca Francis, Thomas Delacourt, Alex Ansdell, Cara Mahoney, Andrew Mayor, Kumiko Mendl, Arno Van Zelst, Patrick Toomey, Prosper Jemmett, Katrina Michaels, Saqib Javaid and Rebekah Murrell. Thanks to Wildcard Theatre for providing space, Em Stott for making it happen and GH Zonana for his assistance.

Special thanks to Mark Evans for his unfailing support in research and Bronte Tadman, for playfully embodying Shakespeare's work and for her contribution to the book.

Thanks to all those who have contributed on Facebook, both at Friends and Alumni of Ecole Jacques Lecoq, and Lecoq and Shakespeare, particularly, Lucien MacDougall, Phelim McDermott, La Gorlinga, Leah Fletcher, Nigel Muson, Patrick Kealey, Simon Murray, Nia Davies, David Gaines, Malcolm Tulip, Michael Newbold, Georgina Sowerby and Jonathan Becker. Thanks to Sadie Jemmett for clues on teaching the four elements freshly and to Saule Ryan for his impish enthusiasm for ensemble games.

Finally, a big thank you to Liz Wilson for letting us film at Oxford School of Drama, to Molly Keogh for performing so well and to Anthony Greyley for shooting and editing the videos with such artistry and efficiency.

INTRODUCTION

Shakespeare and Lecoq may seem unlikely bedfellows. The focus of many practical handbooks on Shakespeare's work is his language, and, in particular, his verse, while Lecoq's work is known for being primarily focused on physicality and movement. As Toby Jones suggests in his foreword, Lecoq's work was premised not on working with text but on finding the need for words – the silence that precedes them. However, as this book will demonstrate, the work of Shakespeare and Lecoq overlaps in many and sometimes unexpected ways, particularly with regard to shared origins in ancient forms of drama and in ways of thinking about the world in elemental terms. Their work shares many points of focus and interest – animal, metallic, mineral and colour imagery to describe human behaviour; an understanding of the emotions in terms of passions; the use of stock figures as a basis for character development, and, perhaps most obviously, the centrality of the figure of the clown (or *bouffon*).

This book is intended to guide the reader through the sort of process that might be undertaken to mount a Shakespeare production or scene study – from warming up to ensemble development , exploring the story and the world of the play, working on the language, character and staging – using Lecoq's techniques to illuminate Shakespeare's rich and varied work. It is, of course, by no means the only way of tackling this process; however, it is one which encourages the actor and student to be creative, imaginative and above all playful; to move away from intellectualizing about the text and instead to allow the body and its instincts to take the lead. Sometimes the work will seem to come from left field or to work against the obvious ways of approaching a scene or character. This is deliberate, and if you trust it, and engage fully with it, it will reap benefits, as many generations of Lecoq actors have discovered.

Lecoq

Jacques Lecoq, world-renowned movement teacher, was born in 1921 in France.

In 1956, he opened the Ecole Internationale de Théâtre Jacques Lecoq, where he taught until his death in 1999. Even after his death, the school continues to thrive and to train theatre practitioners from around the world. Lecoq's techniques now form a significant part of the movement instruction in drama schools around the world.

As Simon Murray asserts, Lecoq was

> a central figure in a loose movement of practitioners, teachers and theorists who proposed that it is the actor's body – rather than simply the spoken text – which is the crucial generator of meaning (s) in theatre. (2018: 3)

It is worth pausing over Murray's statement for a moment. Most practitioners, teachers and theorists would probably assert that an actor needs to use their body alongside the text in order to truly inhabit a character. However, Lecoq's work moves beyond this, foregrounding the body and its movement and focusing on the external (movement) as a way of influencing the internal (feelings), rather than the other way around.

As Murray writes:

> Lecoq's work has two fundamental principles:
>
> - Movement provokes emotion
> - The body remembers
>
> The school believes in a strong link between movement and emotion and avoids any separation between *movement* technique and *acting*. (2018: 129, emphasis in original)

The notion that movement provokes emotion is, in some ways, an obvious one. If we perform a particular movement it can affect how we feel. Skipping around a room, for example, might make us feel happy, while sitting, curled in a ball, rocking back and forth, might quickly make us feel withdrawn and sad.

That the body remembers is also crucial to understanding the link between movement and feeling. Since the body has a physical memory, the emotions generated by a physical action will remain stored in the body. This can be used in quite an abstract way in rehearsal exercises, sometimes in association with text, in a way that later informs performance without the physical action needing to be repeated.

Darren Tunstall describes just such an exercise when writing about the application of Lecoq's work to the Shakespearean text:

> The actors speak the text, performing a physical gesture for each phrase (and sometimes a gesture for each word of the text). These gestures are performed by the whole body, not just the hands; the impulse for a gesture can come from the feet, the knee, the pelvis, the sternum, the nose, the top of the head, and so on. The external forms of some of these gestures may be kept in performance. But where they are not, the actor is encouraged to speak the phrase with the same intonation he or she used when rehearsing the gesture. The influence of the gesture remains, even when the gesture itself is not performed. (2016: 272)

That Lecoq's work can be, and is frequently, applied to the performance of Shakespeare is not in question. However, the process by which this is done has rarely been written about and still less systematized in a way that is useful for actors and directors in a rehearsal room.

This book seeks to provide actors, directors, teachers and students with a clear, practical guide to applying the work of Jacques Lecoq to the process of rehearsing a Shakespeare play or exploring the Shakespearean text in a workshop environment. It takes the reader through a detailed process, beginning with warm-ups and ensemble-building, and moving through explorations of story, the world of the play, the text, character, clowning and *bouffon* and staging.

Lecoq did not write much about his work, apart from the book *Le Corps Poetique* (*The Moving Body*, 1999) and some essays in *Le Théâtre du Geste* (*The Theatre of Movement and Gesture*, 1987). However, his work has had a wide influence, spread by those he has taught. One of Lecoq's most influential pupils, later a teacher at the Ecole Jacques Lecoq, was Philippe Gaulier. Having trained with Lecoq in the 1960s and taught at the school in the 1970s,

Gaulier set up his own school – Ecole Philippe Gaulier – in 1980, building his work around Lecoq's idea of *le jeu* – play. Another important training school which grew out of the work of Lecoq was LISPA (The London International School of Performing Arts). The school was established in both Berlin and London in 2003 by Thomas Prattki, who was a former 'pedagogical director' at the Ecole Jacques Lecoq, and Amy Russell, who trained with Lecoq in the 1990s.

As Tunstall writes:

Lecoq's repertoire of concepts and exercises has been subjected to continuous revision in the hands of those who trained either at his school or with other teachers. (2016: 268)

This is an important point to note when exploring the work of Lecoq, since many of the elements of his training have been adapted by other practitioners, as they have taken ownership of the work and found their own terminology with which to speak about it. Acknowledging some of the difficulties that have arisen from the fact that little of Lecoq's training is written about, and his methods are often passed down by word of mouth, this book aims to unpick some of the methods and the terminology used by various practitioners, in order to provide a clear sense of those which derive directly from the teaching of Lecoq, and those that depart from or draw partially on his work.

Another challenge with Lecoq's work is that it is most frequently written about or put into practice in translation, and the way in which some of the terminology has been translated varies from one practitioner to another. For example, *le jeu* is one of the key concepts of Lecoq's work. This is translated into English as 'play'. This word can have quite frivolous connotations, often something that is childish and lacks serious purpose, or most frequently in the theatre, being used to refer to a written drama. Neither of these definitions accurately captures the work of Lecoq which was neither trivial nor focused around the written text. However, as Mark Evans explains, while *le jeu* and 'play' share certain meanings, *le jeu* 'also suggests a kind of playful creativity that might best be understood by the English word 'improvisation' – an activity and a pedagogic approach at the heart of Lecoq's teaching' (Lecoq, 2000: xviii). This book makes close reference to Lecoq's original French terminology, acknowledging that there is not always a satisfactory direct English translation.

The notion of *le jeu*/play as something infantile or inconsequential is something that this book seeks to dispel, particularly when it comes to performing Shakespeare. Indeed, we argue that the more 'playful' you are, in the full sense of the word, the more 'playfully' you investigate a role, scene or speech; and the more physically motivated that 'playfulness' is, the more vital and lifelike your acting of Shakespeare will be.

The Lecoq training

The Ecole Jacques Lecoq still thrives today and trains theatre practitioners from all over the world. The training is, initially, a one-year programme, after which around a third of the student cohort is invited to remain for a second year.

During the first year of training students study analysis of movement, improvisation, group creation and '*transposition*' – the art of channelling observations of the real world into movement. In the second year they progress, practising various styles of theatre from Commedia Dell'Arte to melodrama, through tragedy to satire and finally to clowning and comedy. Importantly, this work is not only aimed at actors. Designed to arouse creativity it is equally applicable to directors, writers and designers.

Lecoq and Shakespeare

The Lecoq training engages little with Shakespeare directly and very little with the Shakespearean text. The only exception to this is clown work, during which, in an exercise focused on 'Clowns putting on a play', Lecoq would often make direct reference to the mechanicals in *A Midsummer Night's Dream*. This connection between Lecoq's clowns and Shakespeare's clowns is explored by Sara Romersberger in 'Lecoq's Clown and Its Application to Playing Shakespeare's Clowns' (2016) and by Dave Peterson in '"Thus, Like the Formal Vice": Mark Rylance and Clowning in *Richard III*' (2020) and will be discussed in full in Chapter 8 of this book, where we explore the affinities between Shakespeare's clowns and fools and Lecoq's clowns and *bouffons*.

In spite of his lack of direct engagement with the Shakespearean text, Lecoq was clearly interested in the work of Shakespeare, and his methods can be seen as having a close connection to Shakespeare in terms of shared influences, interests and use of imagery.

The work of both Shakespeare and Lecoq is profoundly influenced by the classical theatre of Ancient Greece and Rome. Shakespeare is likely to have attended an Elizabeth Grammar school, where he would have received a humanist education, focused predominantly on Latin texts, including the plays of Seneca, Plautus and Terence. The influence of this education can be seen in the language, plots and characters of his plays. Classical Latin drama was itself influenced by the drama of Ancient Greece and one can trace a direct line from the 'stock figures' of the New Greek Comedies of Menander, which feature social types such as young lovers, stern fathers, boastful soldiers and crafty slaves, through those of Plautus's Roman comedies to Shakespeare's plays (most notably *The Comedy of Errors*, which is based directly on two plays by Plautus – *Menaechmi* and *Amphituro*). A similar line of influence can be traced from Greek tragedy, through the Roman plays of Seneca to Shakespeare's own tragic drama in terms of themes, characterization and language.

Greek tragedy also played a prominent role in Lecoq's training methods. In 1960, he travelled to the Greek Theatre at Syracuse to work on Euripides' *Ion and Hecuba* (Lust, 2000: 108). Lecoq's published work on tragedy revolves around the figures of the chorus and the hero. However, his conception of the chorus is far from the singing, dancing choruses of the Greek theatre. Rather, using both improvisation and text work, Lecoq outlines exercises in which the chorus is based on a 'crowd' and his hero on a 'orator', who must address the crowd to persuade them of the importance of his cause and is then followed by a second orator 'who contradicts the first by arguing the opposite case' (Lecoq, 135–7). This is a scenario common to many of Shakespeare's plays, most obviously *Julius Caesar* in which both Brutus and Antony in turn address the crowd. It also links to some of the training in classical oratory and rhetoric that Shakespeare would have received in school, and which influences his writing of such scenes. As Lecoq explains, 'The birth of the chorus begins with one of the finest exercises devised at the school: "balancing the stage"' (Lecoq, 2000: 141). Lecoq describes with great precision, the ways in which different groups, of different sizes, can balance the space, describing the exercise as 'the fundamental exercise for productions' (Lecoq, 2000: 143). This chorus exercise – *Le Plateau* – is explored in Chapter 9 of this book, where we present ways of exploring how to stage a Shakespeare production – from scenes involving only one or two actors to those involving large crowds.

It should, of course, be acknowledged that Shakespeare's drama itself features choric figures – the choruses in *Henry V* and *Romeo and Juliet*, Time in *The Winter's Tale*, Rumour in *2 Henry IV*, the Prologue/Epilogues in *Troilus and Cressida* and *Henry VIII* and Gower in *Pericles*. These figures are less indebted to the choruses of Classical Greek drama than to the narrator or prologue figures of the medieval drama, being single figures who guide the audience through narrative and temporal gaps in the drama. Nevertheless, as we explore in Chapter 9, some productions of Shakespeare's plays (in particular those influenced by the work of Lecoq) choose to have the chorus speeches delivered by the ensemble and, as such, may benefit from Lecoq's work on choral delivery and movement.

A direct lineage from classical Roman theatre to Commedia Dell'Arte remains a matter of some debate. However, there are clear parallels between the two forms, particularly in terms of the stock characters. In Roman comedy these include the *senex* (old man), *miles gloriosus* (braggart soldier), the *matrona* (mother and wife) and the young lovers; in Commedia the *zannis, vecchi* (old men, including *Il Dottore* (the doctor, a pedant) and *Pantalone* (the pantaloon)), *Il Capitano* (the braggart soldier) and *innamorati* (the lovers). David Rudlin argues that 'the Commedia troupes' (professional, masked outdoor theatre troupes) 'adopted' a great deal of their material from the *commedia erudita* (acted by amateur dilettanti, scripted and performed without the mask and in elaborate costume on the private indoor stages of the courts), which, 'in turn, attempted little which did not derive from Plautus and Terrence' (1994: 14–16).

Lecoq first encountered Commedia in late 1947 when he joined *Les Comediens de Grenoble*, but his interest was cemented the following year when he began work at the University of Padua. Lecoq took Commedia back to his school in Paris, but worried that the form had been reduced in some people's minds to cliché, he instead used the term '*la comédie humaine*' (the human comedy) in order to widen the field of reference (Lecoq, 2000: 113–14). For Lecoq, Commedia revolved around 'the great trickeries of human nature: persuading people, duping them, taking advantage' and, when 'pushed to its extreme', revealed 'the tragedy that lies buried beneath it' (Lecoq, 2000: 114).

Lecoq cites Shakespeare as one of the dramatists whose work shows the influence of the Commedia (2000: 123), and these features of human behaviour – cheating, enticing, deceiving and exploiting – can be seen in a number of Shakespeare's plays, both comedies and tragedies. Some apparent similarities between Shakespeare and Commedia may be the result of their shared heritage in Roman comedy; however, we know that Commedia companies visited England in the sixteenth century, and some references in Shakespeare's work suggest that he was familiar with the form: Lucentio, in *The Taming of the Shrew*, for example, refers to Gremio as 'the old pantaloon' (3.1.36), a figure also invoked by Jaques in *As You Like It* (2.7.159); Don Armado in *Love's Labour's Lost* is referred to in the Folio stage directions as '*Braggart*' (TLN.2466) and Holofernes as '*Pedant*' (TLN.1150). A number of critics have identified parallels between Shakespeare's characters and comic scenarios and those of the Commedia. Further, as Artemis Preeshl has shown, irrespective of how much influence Shakespeare drew directly from the Commedia, elements of Commedia have been inserted into many productions of the plays (2017).

In Chapter 6, we explain the links between Lecoq's work on 'Leading with Different Parts of the Body' and the Commedia, and in Chapter 7 we draw on Lecoq's work on Commedia when exploring an embodiment of the passions.

A further link between Shakespeare and Lecoq can be seen in the shared imagery prominent in both of their work in relation to human behaviour and emotions. As Claudia Sachs explains, the training at the Lecoq school employs 'elements . . . materials, colours, lights, animals . . . which later can become physical possibilities for building human characters' (2016: 53). This notion that various aspects of the natural world can be directly related to human thought and feeling runs through Shakespeare's writing in his use of metaphor, simile and personification.

Animal imagery abounds in Shakespeare's work, with many characters described as having animalistic traits. In *King Lear*, for example, Albany refers to Goneril and Regan as 'tigers' (4.2.41) and Goneril as a 'gilded serpent' (5.3.85). Lear calls Goneril 'detested kite' (1.4.254). Richard III is described by Queen Margaret within a single scene as a 'rooting hog' (1.3.227), 'poisonous bunchback'd toad' (1.3.245), 'dog' (1.3.215) and 'bottled spider' (1.3.241). These are, of course, insults and cannot be taken at face value, but they provide a vivid sense of some of the inner and outer qualities of these characters as perceived by others and can provide stimulus for actors playing the roles. We explore the use of animal studies as a means of creating character in Chapter 7.

Materials such as metals, stone and liquids also feature regularly in imagery describing characters and their emotions. Henry V, for example, describes himself as 'created with a stubborn outside, with an aspect of iron' (5.2), Prince Hal calls Falstaff 'This oily rascal' (*1 Henry IV*, 2.4) and Olivia in *Twelfth Night* speaks of Cesario as 'a heart of stone' (3.4). Colour and elemental images also feature regularly in relation to emotion. Corin in *As You Like It* describes Phoebe's demeanour as 'the red glow of scorn and proud disdain' while Paulina in *The Winter's Tale* speaks of her own anger as 'red-looked' (2.2). These images mesh closely with Lecoq's views about the emotional characteristics of the colour red, which he describes in his book as leading students to 'make explosive movements' (46). Indeed, as Lecoq observes, particular colours seem to provoke the same sorts of movements irrespective of country or culture (46). We explore the embodiment of colour in Chapter 4, when we explore what Lecoq called the 'universal poetic awareness' (2000: 47). As Mark Evans explains, this is 'a process through which movement and gesture can develop and extend meaning and significance beyond the literal and towards the profound' (Lecoq, 2000: 47–8).

In terms of elements, we find the words 'airy', 'earthy', 'fiery' and 'watery' used regularly in Shakespeare to describe characters. Colours and elements are, of course, both closely bound up with the early modern notion of the humours as defining temperament. As we explore in some detail in Chapter 6, the early moderns believed that the body was comprised of four humours and that the way in which these were balanced in the body dictated someone's personality, health, feelings and actions. Ayse Tashkiran, Lecoq-trained movement director who has worked on a number of Shakespeare productions at the RSC, writes about her own use of 'the metaphoric potential of the material world that underpins

Elizabethan cosmology', asserting that a 'humoral reading of a character can open up movement potential': 'I translate the metaphoric into actionable movement activities that contribute to the actor's embodied imagination for the purpose of character' (2016: 231–2).

In early modern understandings of emotion, the humours were strongly linked to the passions, which were, as Hoffman explains, 'experienced as humoural shifts within the body' (2014: 174). Passions were 'the vocabulary used to define feeling in the early modern period' (Hultquist, 2017: 71). The passions were experienced not only in the mind but in the body – as a physiological phenomenon. The term 'passion' is also used by Lecoq in *The Moving Body*, where he talks about students studying 'the human passions from jealousy to pride' (2000: 165) and includes an image of students physically embodying the passions (2000: 163). In Chapter 7, we explore the eleven passions identified by Thomas Aquinas in his *Summa Theologiae* of 1485, embodying them physically and finding the rhythms that underlie them.

The other obvious connection between the work of Lecoq and Shakespeare comes through the wide application of Lecoq's work to the plays of Shakespeare through those who trained at the Ecole Jacques Lecoq, including:

- Actor Steven Berkoff (whose work includes *Shakespeare's Heroes and Villains*) and *Coriolanus*;
- Actor Geoffrey Rush, who has acted extensively in Shakespeare productions;
- Director Julie Taymor, whose work includes the film *Titus* (1999), productions of *The Tempest* (on stage and screen) and a stage production of *A Midsummer Night's Dream* (2013);
- Movement director Jane Gibson, who was head of Movement at the NT from 1999 to 2009, and has also worked for the RSC, the Almeida and Cheek by Jowl;
- Movement director Ayse Tashkiran, associate artist at the RSC;
- Director James McDonald, who has directed *Love's Labour's Lost* (1992) and *Richard II* (1993) (Manchester Royal

Exchange), *The Tempest* (RSC, 2000) and *King Lear* (Public Theatre, New York, 2011);

- Simon McBurney, Annabel Arden, Fiona Gordon and Marcello Magni, founders of Théâtre de Complicité;
- Ariane Mnouchkine, founder of the Théâtre du Soleil.

The work of the theatre companies Théâtre du Soleil and Théâtre de Complicité features extensively throughout this book, as does that of the companies Footsbarn Travelling Theatre and Flabbergast Theatre.

- Théâtre du Soleil was founded in 1964 by Ariane Mnouchkine and fellow students from the Ecole Internationale de Théâtre Jacques Lecoq. The company is 'known for its collaboratively created productions that examine the social impact of politics events', and for its *mise en scene,* which 'is broadly influenced by popular traditional European theatre forms such as the Commedia Dell'arte and puppetry, as well as Asian traditional theatre' (Richardson, 2019: 81). Between 1968 and 2015 Theatre du Soleil produced a number of Shakespeare's plays, including *A Midsummer Night's Dream, Richard II* and *Henry IV*, Parts 1 and 2, *The Comedy of Errors* and *Macbeth*.
- Théâtre de Complicité was founded in 1983 by Annabel Arden, Fiona Gordon, Marcello Magni and Simon McBurney. As McBurney has written, the work of the company 'has its roots in the shared training of its members at the Jacques Lecoq School in Paris' (quoted in Fry, 2015: 167). In 2000 the name of the company was changed to Complicité, and it is this name that we use throughout the book, for the sake of ease. The company's focus is on collaboration and devising. It has created a number of adaptations of classical texts, including *The Winter's Tale* (1992) and *Measure for Measure* (2004).
- Footsbarn Travelling Theatre was founded in 1971 by Oliver Foot and John Paul Cook, the latter of whom had trained with Jacques Lecoq, with the aim to 'create a form of theatre that was popular, generous and accessible to all' (Footsbarn, 2023). Originally established in Cornwall, the company

relocated to France in 1991. They have produced a number of Shakespeare plays, including '*A Midsummer Night's Dream*, first produced in 1976, *Romeo and Juliet*, *Macbeth*, *The Winter's Tale*, *The Tempest*' and 'medleys such as *Incomplete Plays* or *Shakespeare Celebration*' (Valls-Russell, 2018: 118–19).

Flabbergast Theatre was formed in 2010, making 'exciting theatre rooted in physicality and devising' (Flabbergast, 2010). The company, led by Henry Maynard, takes its lead in movement matters partially from the Lecoq-trained associates, Simon Gleave and Briony O'Callaghan.

We will refer regularly throughout the book to the work of all of these companies, since they provide clear examples of Lecoq's work being used successfully to create imaginative, physical, ensemble productions of Shakespeare's work.

Although limited attention has been given in critical writing to the application of Lecoq's methods to Shakespeare, in addition to Sarah Romersberger's article, cited earlier, the *Routledge Companion to Jacques Lecoq* contains an essay by Darren Tunstall entitled 'Lecoq and Shakespeare' in which Tunstall draws on the work of Ariane Mnouchkine and Complicité, as well as his own productions, to argue that Lecoq's ideas can be usefully applied to the Shakespearean text.

The main element on which Tunstall focuses is the importance of the audience in the work of Lecoq and Shakespeare. For him, the work of Lecoq makes the actor 'more attuned to the audience' and 'is one of the great gifts of Lecoq's pedagogy for any artist seeking to bring to the public a renewed and invigorated sense of Shakespeare's value' (2016: 273). This is undoubtedly true, and this book will repeatedly show how under Lecoq's influence, the emphasis shifts from the individual actor to the collective effect on the audience.

However, it will also seek to demonstrate that the work of Lecoq can be productively applied at all stages of a rehearsal process for a Shakespeare play, enriching a sense of place, story and character. Each chapter addresses a different aspect of performance, suggesting exercises that can be pursued by an individual or a group, as part of the preparation of a full production or for workshops, scene studies and monologues.

This book

It is important to say that the premise of this book is to explore ways in which Lecoq's techniques can be marshalled to the service of a rehearsal process for a Shakespeare play. It does not seek to detail how a Lecoq-trained company might mount a Shakespeare play, since this is difficult to pin down, and is likely to venture into the realm of adaptation.

Most workshops and days of rehearsal begin with exercises designed to warm up the voice, body and imagination and to encourage focus. Shakespeare's plays are physically and vocally demanding. They also require actors to use their creativity and imagination, as they work out, together, how to tell the story of the play and create the world or worlds in which it takes place. As will be discussed in Chapter 1, Lecoq did not believe in undertaking mechanical physical exercises. He believed that all action should be motivated. His warm-ups may begin with mechanical movement, but this is soon expanded out into the space, used to explore the dynamics and the imagery of the drama and extended into breath and voice. Chapter 1, 'Exploring the Body in Space', is essentially a chapter of warm-ups, but each exercise is connected to atmosphere, meaning and emotion. The title of the chapter deliberately reflects Lecoq's interest in space. As Murray writes, 'the pulsating heart of all his work was the human body and its movement in space' (2018: 33). 'Space' is also at the heart of the work carried out at the Laboratoire d'Etude du Mouvement (LEM), a studio adjacent to the Ecole Jacques Lecoq, established in 1976, where many of the first year students have taken classes. LEM has been run by Pascale Lecoq (Lecoq's daughter), who is an architect and stage designer, and Emmauelle Bouyer, architect and plastic artist. Its stated aims are:

- universal discovery of the laws governing movement and spaces

- the creation of dynamic structures

- how to put the human body into space (Ecole Lecoq, 2020).

Another crucial facet of the Lecoq training is the creation of *complicité,* a fact to which the name of the Lecoq-based theatre company Complicité bears testament. As Murray explains, *complicité* 'is critical in the achievement of a true sense of ensemble' (Murray, 2018: 65), although, the English word 'complicity' does not fully encompass the sense of shared playfulness needed between members of a company. The early modern theatre also revolved around a sense of close collaboration and ensemble. It revolved around a series of acting companies, each with a core of actors who remained together for a number of years. Many have argued that this permanence and familiarity was key to the success of productions mounted with limited rehearsal time. A number of modern companies who perform Shakespeare on a regular basis have attempted to emulate some degree of this sense of 'ensemble'. Ideas about the qualities and conditions needed for ensemble to function vary. Some would argue that a degree of permanence is necessary, others a shared set of ideals; however, irrespective of definitions, once any theatre company (or indeed a group of students) is gathered together to work on a play, they will need to find ways of collaborating and cooperating. Chapter 2 sets out a series of exercises designed to encourage listening, openness, flexibility, focus and awareness among a group of actors.

This book suggests that once actors have gained a sense of 'ensemble' the first stage of approaching a Shakespeare play is to explore the story, in order for the whole company to gain an understanding of the plot and structure. While this is often done through a seated read-through of the play, Chapter 3 suggests that it can be achieved through playful, active means. Once the company has explored the story, Chapter 4 provides a range of exercises for examining the world of the play, making use of some of Lecoq's most famous methods: *auto-cours*, which translates as 'self-lesson' and 'refers to the one-and-a-half hours students spend each day at the school working in groups to create performances based on weekly themes given by the teachers' (Gilrain, 2016: 132) and 'Seven Levels of Tension', which has become probably Lecoq's most famous exercise, mediated through multiple practitioners, and here used to explore tension within situations and spaces rather than within individual characters, as is often the case. Finally, in Chapter 4 we explore what Lecoq called 'The universal poetic awareness' – the practical exploration of the rhythms, movements and dynamics of abstract phenomena such as 'spaces, lights, colours, materials, sounds' (Lecoq, 2000: 47).

For many practitioners, the main focus of a rehearsal process for a Shakespeare production is the text. As has already been mentioned, Lecoq's published work does not engage in any detailed way with the Shakespearean text, and the work done specifically on Shakespeare's plays at the school is limited. However, Simon Murray argues that it is a misconception that Lecoq's work does not engage with text at all. As he explains:

> Contrary to what outsiders sometimes imagine, in the second year Lecoq works with students on text, especially in the realms of tragedy and melodrama. When writing about his approach to tragic texts he observes: In our way of working, we enter a text through the body. We never sit around and discuss . . . . My teaching method steers clear of any interpretation, concentrating on the constant respect for the internal dynamics of the text, avoiding all a priori readings. (2018: 47)

Many of Lecoq's strategies provide the actor with tools for exploring the text 'through the body'. Chapter 5, 'Exploring the Text', includes exercises on the use of abstract movement to open up Shakespeare's words, rhetorical and stylistic devices, asides, speeches and dialogue.

Through the text we can examine what a character is saying; however, the actor needs to find ways of embodying these utterances – exploring the underlying thoughts and emotions. Chapters 6 and 7 are concerned with the exploration of character. Chapter 6 is primarily concerned with 'Character Types'. It looks at the early modern humours, as a means of conceiving character, exploring these through a connection to Lecoq's work on the elements. The chapter then extends this work into an exploration of character physicality, through two exercises connected to Commedia – 'Leading with Different Parts of the Body' and 'Pushing and Pulling'. Chapter 7 expands on this archetypal character work, to explore the emotional drives and intentions of characters and the characteristics which define them.

Chapter 8 tackles the specific characters of the Shakespearean clown and the fool, using Lecoq's exercises on play, clowning and *bouffon*. The chapter examines the differences between the clown and the *bouffon*, arguing that the *bouffon* is the closest analogue to the Shakespearean 'fool', while the clown can embrace a range of naïve, childlike, vulnerable and ridiculous figures. We also suggest that while Lecoq's exercises on clowning and *bouffon* may seem most obviously suited to Shakespeare's comic characters, they can be equally valuably employed in the exploration of serious or even tragic characters.

The final chapter provides exercises to assist with the staging of a production, thinking about balancing the stage space, shaping the space, the nature of chorus work and the possibilities and constraints of various spaces.

How to use this book

Each chapter of the book includes a series of exercises. Often we explore a preparatory version of the exercise, before outlining how it might be used in relation to a Shakespeare text. Throughout the book, we draw on selected examples from Shakespeare's work in order to illustrate the exercises presented. We do so in the knowledge and hope that you will apply these to speeches, scenes and productions on which you are working. At times we also make suggestions about the possible outcomes of an exercise. Remember that these are only suggestions. We want you to find your own ways of doing things and, crucially, your own responses.

Throughout the book you will find videos of some of the key exercises described.

1

Exploring the body in space

As indicated in the Introduction, different directors have different ideas about how a rehearsal process for a Shakespeare play might begin. However, irrespective of whether they choose to begin with a traditional read-through or to begin with actors on their feet in the rehearsal room, most will see the need for some form of warm-up activity. Adrian Noble in his book *How to Direct Shakespeare* states: 'On almost every production I direct, in drama and opera, I will get the actors on their feet on the very first day. This may start with a simple warm-up, ideally both physical and vocal' (2022: 157).

In order to be ready to rehearse, the actor needs to have a warm, supple body and a warm, flexible voice. Warm-ups can also help to diffuse 'fear' that actors can bring with them into a rehearsal room. However, Lecoq was not in favour of warm-up exercises done purely in order to exercise or relax the body or indeed to allay fears. He believed that even when warming up, an actor's movement should be motivated and 'justified' (a term we will explore further in this chapter):

In the theatre making a movement is never a mechanical act but must always be a gesture that is justified. Its justification may consist in an indication or an action, or even an inward state. (Lecoq, 2000: 69)

These three areas of indication, action and state will be explored in Exercise 4.

In *The Moving Body* Lecoq describes the various stages of physical warm-ups, to which he gives 'meaning':

1. Carrying out the movement 'mechanically, very simply, in order to see how it goes'
2. Enlarging the movement 'to test its limits, filling the largest possible space'
3. Concentrating 'on two essential phases in the movement, trying to understand their dramatic dynamics' – these being 'the starting point' and 'the end of the movement'
4. Introducing breath into the movement
5. Introducing a 'dramatic dimension' through the use of images
6. Introducing a 'vocal dimension': 'Each gesture possesses its own sonority, or voice, which I try to help the students discover.'

(2000: 70–1)

The exercises in this chapter encompass many of these elements – mechanical movement, expanded movement, movement that focuses on the beginning and end points, breath in movement, drama in movement and voice and movement. It draws in particular on Lecoq's chapter on 'Movement Technique' in *The Moving Body*, exploring notions of 'giving meaning to movement' and 'Movement analysis' – the analysis of physical action, in particular the 'natural movements' of 'undulation' and '*éclosion*' (2000: 75).

We begin with an exercise on 'warming up the space', which may seem unusual, given that you might imagine that the body comes first. However, as explained in the Introduction, this derives directly from Lecoq's teaching, where a movement session would often start with the phrase '*chauffez l'espace*' ('warm up the space') and begins a long journey with the concept of 'space' in the training, which is, by its very nature, invisible to the eye, but palpable none the less.

Warming up the space

Moving freely and noticing changes in your mood

- Move through the room you are in.

- Move faster. Jog. Move slower and take in the space. Try to warm it up in some way. Don't think about how to do this, but do whatever occurs to you: rubbing the walls, moving furniture or even singing. To begin with you are livening up the space around you in any way that you choose.

- Move your arms and legs energetically through the air. By doing so you are warming up the space by making the molecules of air heat up. You are making the air warmer, and, at the same time, reflexively, you are warming your body up too but not thinking about it. You have started a process of playing without self-consciousness.

- Move freely around the space, running, jumping, spinning. Do as you please. Notice how the different activities make you feel. Running has a kind of rush to it, jumping a determination and spinning a sort of giddiness.

Turning improvisation into simple narrative

- Move in a way that is very free. For example:

  1. Go at different speeds.
  2. Run to a wall. Stop.
  3. Creep along the side of the room until you get to the corner. When you get there, turn. Jump up as high as you can and move out into the middle of the room again.
  4. Roll on the floor.

- Spend two or three minutes playing with this kind of free movement. As you are doing it, pay some attention to what you enjoy. At the end of two or three minutes, recall three types of movements. For example:

  1. Jumping and then running and stopping.
  2. Spinning around a few times.
  3. Moving gently through the space simply stimulating the movement of air with your arms out to the sides.

- Make each of these movements into a kind of sequence. Make the three movement sequences as different from one another as possible. Each of these movement sequences has the potential to be expressive. In our examples here, the first – jumping, running and stopping – could contain elements of excitement. The second – the spinning – might speak of a kind of delirium, and the third, with arms out, could be spreading good will.

- See if you can make each movement sequence have a beginning and an ending. However simple, the movement sequence has a kind of story to it. These 'two moments', as detailed earlier, are viewed by Lecoq as the key phases of movement, which 'carry a strong dramatic charge' – the beginning representing a moment of 'risk' and the end a moment of 'landing' and a return to 'calm' (Lecoq, 2000: 70–1).

- Show your movements to one another and contemplate whether the movements 'speak' of something. The human body in motion contains seeds of expression, and those seeds will be transplanted into your work on character, story and text.

Eclosion (hatching)

Eclosion is illustrated by Lecoq in *The Moving Body* (2000: 76). He describes it as one of the 'natural movements which occur in everyday life' (2000: 75). It is a movement which 'opens up from the centre'; 'a global sensation which can be performed in both directions: expanding or contracting' (2000: 78).

- Start by crouching, on the flats of your feet, in a ball-like shape, with your arms crossed over in between your knees. Slowly open up, trying to move your arms, body and legs at the same time and at an even pace, so that you arrive, stood up with your arms extended out to the side, just above the horizontal. This is *éclosion*. Do the same thing in reverse, so that you close, like the petals of a flower, down and in, trying to move arms, legs and body at the same rate until you are crouched over in a kind of ball again.

This is available to watch with Video 1: https://bloomsbury.pub/ shakespeare-and-lecoq

- Split into pairs and watch one another do this. What do you see? Is it more than just a person opening up and closing their body? What is happening to the space around the person doing the movement? Can you see that when they open, the space gets bigger and when they become more ball-like the space contracts?

- Could it be metaphorical? At one level it is a person stretching out and curling up. Can you see beyond this? If so, what do you see or imagine? The changing of the space, as indicated earlier, might be more palpable to your sensation, than visible to the eye.

- Do this movement on your own and let some words come to you inwardly as to how it feels. On opening you may feel vulnerable or hopeful and on closing you may feel precise, constricted or intrigued.

This process of taking a simple movement and investigating it at a more poetic level is known as 'transposition' (Lecoq, 2000: 45). Helen Richardson explains *transposition* as the 'transformation of the real into the theatrical' (2016: 310).

Waking up your spine

L'ondulation or the undulation

Like *éclosion*, undulation is another of the 'natural movements' described by Lecoq and illustrated in *The Moving Body* (2000: 75). He describes it as 'the human being's first movement, the one underlying all locomotion', explaining that it 'takes its leverage from the ground and effort is gradually transmitted to all the parts of the body until it reaches the point of application' (2000: 75, 77).

This exercise is available to watch with Video 2, and you will notice that the actor performing it goes through once slowly, then once a bit quicker, and then four times while emphasizing the pulse in the knees, pelvis, chest and head in turn: https://bloomsbury.pub/shakespeare-and-lecoq

- Stand with your feet under your hip joints or about shoulder-width apart. Imagine a see-through wall or plate of glass coming vertically up from the front of your feet.

- Lean your head and body forwards, with back fairly straight, and arms hanging down through the imagined glass, with your legs straight. Keep looking ahead.

- When your legs feel like they need to bend, bend your knees, round your back and look to the ground. Your knees will shoot forwards through the imaginary glass plate and your body will curl fully and then start to uncurl. Keep your arms heavy and hanging towards the ground all through this exercise.

- As you uncurl upwards, bring your pelvis forwards so that it touches the imaginary glass plate in front of you. Let your head and eyes come naturally up towards the horizon as you uncurl.

- Push your chest forwards towards the imaginary glass plate while keeping your head back, but your face forwards; this is tricky.

- Finally bring your face towards the imaginary glass plate and carry on so that the head comes forward and you lean forwards, letting your bottom stick out and your arms hang down as you repeat the cycle. It is a wave.

It may take some time to get used to the movement, so take rests while learning it. Also, as you bring your pelvis forwards, tighten your buttocks a bit to give your lower back some support.

- Keep your feet as flat to the floor as you can while you do this and learn to do it with ease.

- Make it smooth, emphasizing the coming forward of the knees, the pelvis, the chest and the face equally. As with *éclosion,* in the previous exercise, you are doing something complicated and demanding while staying calm which is a skill that will be helpful to you as you negotiate the complexities of Shakespeare's writing, while maintaining the kind of 'smoothness' that Hamlet speaks of in his advice to the players (*Ham.*3.2.5-8).

- When you feel confident that you have created this undulation up through your body, from your feet to your knees, through your pelvis and chest up to your head and down again, start to put more power into it. Push your knees forward through the imaginary wall more forcefully and allow the resulting power to surge up through your spine as it snakes its way up. Be careful not to let your head tip back when the wave reaches your neck. In this movement, you are seeking to get your face as open to the space in front of you (the space of the audience and not the sky) as soon as possible.

- Split into pairs and watch one another do the movement. The undulation that Lecoq teaches is one of a human being losing connection momentarily with the space in front of them as they go down, and then finding it again. The face, although inexpressive, is very important, here, in signalling both to the actor and to the spectator that a connection is being made.

Lecoq links the 'four main body-positions' of the undulation – inclined forwards, drawn up to its full height, inclined backwards and hunched – to the different ages of life: 'infancy, adulthood, maturity and old age', suggesting that the forward position suggests 'the image of childhood', the vertical position 'the mature adult', the backwards inclination to 'the autumn of life' and hunching to 'old age' (2000: 77–8). These are, of course, all phases of life invoked by Shakespeare in Jaques famous 'Seven Ages of Man' speech in *As You Like It* (2.7.140-167), and we find characters of all these types in Shakespeare's plays.

Grounding

When discussing work on the four elements – air, water, earth and fire – Lecoq describes 'the tree' as 'most important for the actor to work at' since this allows him to be grounded, or 'positively planted in the ground' (2000: 44). This section of the exercise is designed to help the actor to feel rooted. We will cover the tree itself in Chapter 6.

- Go back to doing the undulation on your own and feel how the movement grows from the ground upwards. You need your feet well planted on the floor to feel this.
- Imagine that while you are doing the same movement, at whatever tempo you like, that you are gathering something from the earth. Decide for yourself; maybe it is an idea, hope

or energy, and as you undulate upwards, it comes out into the space in front of you as your face appears and you fall forwards again.

- Imagine that you are a wave. As the water approaches the beach, it rises and then the white top topples forwards and down. You are a wave, building up and plummeting down on to the beach.

- See if you can build up a sense of resistance as you make your wave come up, so that you delay the moving forward of your face into the space, as if you are holding something back. It will give you a feeling of being in control, as if you, the actor, can control how your energy is to be shared.

Connecting to Shakespeare

- Think of a line of text from the play you are working on and imagine gathering it up from the ground with the undulation. From standing you lean over forwards, you bend your knees and your gaze falls groundward. As you gather the line of text, you build up impetus and you snake upwards. Then as your chest comes forward and up, you let the line of text come out of you. Stand tall and stop the head from coming forwards this time. Let the breath, sounds and words come into the space you create in front of you.

- Repeat this several times until you feel how you can time your surging upwards with the release of the line.

- Do this same thing with increasingly long lines of text and see how much energy you can gather from the ground, in this way, to give impetus to increasingly complex spoken thoughts.

Movement with meaning

In this exercise you will be introduced to gravity, muscle release, sensuousness, suspension and play.

All bodily movement in the theatre contains some meaning. The task of the actor is to be aware enough of what they are doing so that they can help to create meaning for the audience as effortlessly as possible.

Swinging the arms

- Find a place to stand.
- Place your feet about a foot's length apart.
- Allow your knees to be very lightly bent or softened.
- Bring your arms forward and let them swing back. Do this several times. Almost feel like you are throwing your arms forward and see if they will swing back behind your body.
- Allow this to continue. You will have to make an effort around your shoulders to get the arms in motion but see if you can let your arms feel heavy.
- After a while, you may sense that your knees can help the movement. If you bend your knees slightly as the arms are swinging past your body, the movement of slightly bending of the legs will increase the swinging of the arms.

This is a simple but powerful way to recognize how the bottom half of your body can help the top half. The whole body is involved in acting.

Exploring with pleasure

- Carry on swinging your arms higher and higher in front of you until they come up almost above your head.
- Allow yourself to look up as the arms get to a point almost directly above your head.
- Notice how it feels to fling your arms up in front of you. Does it give you some pleasure? Can there be some joy in it? Do not feel the need to generate the joy but see if the actual movement of the arms swinging creates it. The movement may contain many emotions: hope, aspiration, freedom. See for yourself what feeling is aroused by the raising of the arms in this way.

This is one of the key teachings from Lecoq: the body contains or stores emotion. Movement releases it or brings it to the surface. As Lecoq explains:

> Each emotive state leaves traces within us and these lay down 'physical circuits' which stay in our memory. That is where the impulses that will turn into gestures, attitudes and movements are organised. (2006: 6)

Suspension

As mentioned earlier, Lecoq links suspension with the beginning and end of a movement – viewing it as linked explicitly to the point at which 'drama' occurs (2000: 71).

- Swing your arms again in this way, and now pay attention to what happens at the top of the swing. The arms must for a moment be stationary to change direction. This is a moment of suspension.
- What does the moment of suspension feel like to you?
- Could you extend the moment of suspension?
- Is it possible that there is a kind of story there? In its most basic form, stories work by asking us to think about what will or will not happen next.
- Could you make believe that maybe the arms won't even come back down . . .? See if that gives you pleasure. It is a kind of play.

Connecting to Shakespeare

As we will discuss in more detail in Chapter 5, much of the dialogue in Shakespeare is in written in verse. There is no universally accepted way in which to speak Shakespeare's verse. Some respected theatre practitioners, however, including Peter Hall, John Barton, Kristin Linklater and Adrian Noble, encourage actors, in their writing, to create a moment of suspension at the end of each line of verse (Hall, 2003: 12; Barton, 1984: 35; Linklater, 1992: 159; Noble, 2009: 69), arguing that this can provide an insight into the thoughts and feelings of the character and can replicate natural patterns of phrasing and breathing. You may find it useful to feel how you can create a tiny moment of suspension at the end of each verse line by using the arm swings.

Here is Salerio at the beginning of *The Merchant of Venice* offering up some reasons as to why his friend, Antonio, is so sad:

> Your mind is tossing on the ocean (*Arms up*)
> There where your argosies with portly sail (*Arms up*)
> Like signiors and rich burghers on the flood, (*Arms up*)
> Or as it were the pageants on the sea, (*Arms up*)
> Do overpeer the petty traffickers (*Arms up*)
> That cur'sy to them, do them reverence, (*Arms up*)
> As they fly by them with their woven wings.
>
> *The Merchant of Venice* (1.1.8-14)

- Try this now. Go over the lines and raise your arms at the end of each verse line. It will challenge your desire to speak the words with grammatical sense, and introduce something of the way that this character, Salerio, is thinking his way through what he has to say.

In life, we don't always know exactly what we are going to say, and this arm swing exercise helps to develop an embodied sense of being in the moment on stage and letting the verse lines breathe.

Connecting movement to emotion

This exercise introduces you to more free movement, and the connection of this movement to feeling, sensation and emotion. Lecoq often talked of 'justifying' a movement. He did not mean 'justification' in any kind of moral sense but in a psycho-physical sense – the movement coming from an emotional or psychological impulse: 'There should be no sense of the body "getting in the way", nor of it feeding parasitically off what it should be conveying. Its foundation is dramatic gymnastics, in which every gesture, every attitude or movement is justified' (Lecoq, 2000: 70).

Spin around.

- Find a space. Take a moment to stand with your feet about a foot's length apart.

- Spin around. Do it a few times.
- What kind of feeling or emotion does it create? Try it at different speeds and you will find that the movement, even when done quite neutrally to start with, creates a feeling, or emotion. Disorientation? Excitement? Fear? Beyond these, how can you 'justify' it?

Jump up.

- If you simply jump and land you will notice a kind of drama appears. Are you trying to reach something? Could it be that you feel surprised, so surprised that you jump in the air? Can you justify a jump with an emotion – not simply an action but more of an emotional justification? It will stretch your capacity to be truthful; this is the challenge of 'justification'.

Stand on one leg.

- Notice how that makes you feel. It may destabilize you, as if injured. But equally it may elevate you, like a dancer or flamingo.
- If you bring your foot and leg away from the floor in several different ways, quickly, slowly, straight up or out to the side, you will feel different emotions, however slight, connected to each of the versions. Name them if you can. For instance, 'surprised', 'suspicious', 'military' and 'comical'. Be inspired by how your movement can create different feelings in you.

Playing Shakespeare with its long thoughts, complex language and often fantastical stories can ask a huge amount of the actor's imagination. It is like an enormous dare which the actor's playfulness must fill. Along with soaring romance, ludicrous hilarity and terrifying behaviour, there is athleticism, virtuosity and play in the Shakespearean world. These moments all need to be addressed and justified emotionally to make them truthful to the audience. The Shakespearean actor is faced with monumental emotional, psychological and verbal challenges, and must then justify them with their imaginative connection.

As mentioned earlier, when talking about justification, Lecoq lays out three main kinds of movement. The first is an **indication,** the second, an **action** and the third a **state** (2000: 69). He explains the three types of movement as follows: 'I raise my arm, to indicate a place or point something out [**indication**], to take an object off a shelf [**action**], or just because an inner emotion makes me feel like raising it [**state**]' (2000: 69).

The spinning around, the jump and the standing on one leg could be any of the three types.

The 'spinning around' could be

> (a) an **indication** – an instruction in a dance class
>
> (b) an **action** – an attempt to see what is going on all around you
>
> (c) a **state** – a spontaneous swirl of delight at good news.

The 'jump' could be

> (a) an **indication** – to someone that they need to jump themselves
>
> (b) an **action** – an effort to see over something
>
> (c) a **state** – an impulsive eruption upwards of joy or fear.

The 'standing on one leg' could be

> (a) an **indication** – showing someone how to balance
>
> (b) an **action** – seeing what is on the bottom of one of your shoes
>
> (c) a **state** – kicking the air with the other foot in triumph.

- Try all the these, spinning, jumping and standing on leg, in the three ways we have suggested.

- Think about the play you are working on. As an actor, use the three suggestions: spinning, jumping and standing on one foot, in relation to some moment from the play that you are working on. This could involve doing the two things simultaneously, like making an entrance as Claudius, in Act 1, Scene 2, of *Hamlet* while spinning around, standing on one foot or jumping. It will take you away from your preconceived idea of how the entrance should be done but may lay the foundations for a better idea. This is a perfect example of what Lecoq means by 'justified'.

- Try some lines with the same three movements – spinning, standing on one leg, and jumping (one after the other) to open up the possibilities of how some of your lines might be approached.

Here is an example. Imagine you are playing Juliet in *Romeo and Juliet*. She has just met and fallen in love with Romeo and the Nurse has just told her that Romeo is a Montague, her family's sworn enemies:

> My only love sprung from my only hate,
> Too early seen unknown, and known too late!
> Prodigious birth of love it is to me
> That I must love a loathed enemy.
>
> (*RJ*, 1.5.137-140)

The following are explorations and not meant as interpretations of the text. Some of them will work better than others, and some or all of them can be explored fully in body movement, and then reduced so that only the trace of the body movement remains with the actor who can then use it as an inspiration.

Spinning around.

- (a) as an **indication** – perhaps she spins around to refer the Nurse back to the moment she and Romeo were dancing together.
- (b) as an **action** – she may be looking for somewhere to go to sit down and contemplate what has just happened.
- (c) as a **state** – she is dazed and spins without even knowing why.

Jumping up.

- (a) as an **indication** – she may be indicating to the Nurse that she is happy.
- (b) as an **action** – she may be jumping up in order to show the Nurse, her new-found love as his head disappears among the crowd.
- (c) as a **state** – she may be jumping up (and down) to expel the new realization.

Standing on one leg.

> (a) as an **indication** – it could be that she is showing the Nurse how unbalanced she feels.
>
> (b) as an **action** – it could be more that she takes one leg off the floor in readiness to go and find someone.
>
> (c) as a **state** – her foot comes of the floor, her knee bends almost in the agony of the realization and maybe she even hugs her own knee.

As we have suggested earlier, some of these don't seem to fit. That is part of their power. They may inspire things in the actor that cannot appear through thinking or analysing the text. Not only can using these movements (and you, of course, will find your own) give direction on how something is played but can also open up new ways of thinking about the play itself.

Sending your voice into the space

The fishing net

This exercise introduces the connection of movement to space and into voice. As cited earlier, linking gesture and voice is one of the stages of the Lecoq warm-up. As he explains:

> Each gesture possesses its own sonority, or voice, which I try to help the students discover. The utterance of a voice in space shares the same nature as the execution of a gesture: just as I can throw a discus in a stadium, I can throw my voice in space. (2000: 71)

- Imagine that you have a fishing net in your hands. It is of manageable size for one person to fling it into the water.

- Imagine water in front of you.

- Mime picking up the fishing net. Feel its weight. Handle it in a way that feels like you are getting control of it in readiness to launch it out into the water.

- Take your arms to the side and then behind you, holding the imagined net, and twist your body around to the front to sling the mass of string and rope netting out over the water.

- Watch the net spread over the water. Stay with it in your gaze as it sinks down to find the fish.

- Try it again. Can you throw the net a bit further? Could you launch it higher? Could you imagine it spreading wider?

- Continue to practice this and add some sound. Make it simple: an 'OH' or 'AH' sound. See if you can make the sound last as long as possible, while linking the sound to the flight of the net.

- Now say your name instead of just 'OH' or 'AH'.

- Then say, 'I am [insert name].'

- Grow it to 'My name is [insert name]'.

- Say progressively longer sentences: 'My name is [insert name] and I am throwing a fishing net'; 'My name is [name] and I am throwing a fishing net into the sea'; 'My name is [name] and I am throwing a heavy fishing net into the lake'.

The great thing about the **fishing net** exercise is that once you have done it, it will be there for you in an embodied way when you come to 'throw' a line across the space, or 'launch' a thought on a breath or on voice into the audience.

- Try a number of Shakespeare's lines with the fishing net , adding another line each time and connecting imaginatively to the preparation, the heaving, the flying, the landing and the sinking of the net.

- Reach down to gather your imagined net, and then as you are launching it, you say:

To be, or not to be – that is the question.

- Once you have done that you reach down and gather the net again and do two lines, and repeat this, adding a line each time, until you feel that you can throw the net, imagine it flying, landing and sinking even starting to gather fish as you say the longest of the following lines.

To be, or not to be – that is the question;
Whether 'tis nobler in the mind to suffer

To be, or not to be – that is the question;
Whether 'tis nobler in the mind to suffer
The slings and arrows of outrageous fortune

To be, or not to be – that is the question;
Whether 'tis nobler in the mind to suffer
The slings and arrows of outrageous fortune
Or to take arms against a sea of troubles

To be, or not to be – that is the question;
Whether 'tis nobler in the mind to suffer
The slings and arrows of outrageous fortune
Or to take arms against a sea of troubles
And by opposing end them.

(Ham. 3.1.55-59)

2

Exploring the ensemble

The concept of 'ensemble' is a somewhat elusive one. John Britton cites the question 'Ensemble – what is "it"?' as 'a simple, unanswerable question' (2013: 4). And yet, the word 'ensemble' is frequently employed in close connection to both the work of Shakespeare and of Lecoq.

The First Folio of *The Workes of William Shakespeare,* published in 1623, contains a list of 'The Names of the Principall Actors in all these Playes' – including William Shakespeare himself. All the players listed were members of the Lord Chamberlain/King's Men, a number for over twenty years (see Gurr, 2004: 217–46). This semi-permanent ensemble with its core of leading actors is often cited as one of the reasons why the Globe Theatre was able to stage multiple plays over a short period of time.

Of course, the way in which the theatre operates as a profession has changed a great deal since the early modern period, and yet the notion of 'ensemble' working, as something that is of benefit in producing Shakespeare's plays on the stage, remains a potent one. When Michelle Terry became artistic director of Shakespeare's Globe in 2018, she introduced the idea of the 'Globe Ensemble', 'inspired by the ways early modern companies created their work':

We know that Shakespeare wrote for a company of artists who knew each other intimately, knew the theatres like the back of their hand, and lived alongside and amongst their audience. Shakespeare's Globe – our new, 21st century one – has been inspired by this to form the Globe Ensemble, taking the spirit of a company of artists working together to stage performances of multiple plays, performed in repertory, with actors playing multiple roles across a season. (Shakespeare's Globe, 2018)

Peter Hall was, to an extent, also influenced by the early modern theatre when he established the Royal Shakespeare Company in 1961. His ambition 'to establish the RSC as one of the great international ensemble companies' (Britton, 2013: 122) was partly inspired by the Berliner Ensemble and partly by the theatres of the Renaissance.

As discussed in the Introduction, ensemble also lies at the heart of Lecoq's work. Simon Murray cites 'rapport and *complicité* in the creation of ensemble' as one of the key areas of Lecoq-based study (2018: 5) and Paddy Hayter, of Footsbarn, concurs:

> Lecoq had an instinctive energy to bring people together. He worked with Jacques Copeau and Jean Dasté who both worked in groups that took theatre out into the villages. At the school you spent so much of the time watching others, being the observer, and receiving and feeling the work of others. The way you worked, you were always being fed with other energies and many of us who have been to the school want to hold on to that.

Exploring the space as an ensemble

The first sequence of exercises is predominantly taken from work with Complicité, although the first iteration of the exercise is described by Lecoq in *The Moving Body*:

> A group of students walks about the room, filling the whole space. On a signal, they group themselves into twos, threes, fives, sevens, etc. (2000: 138)

Lecoq suggests the exercise mainly as a way of exploring the dynamics of different groups. Here we suggest its use as a means of creating *complicité* between members of the group; encouraging actors to give their attention to others, and to work collaboratively on a task. We give increasingly complex variations of the exercise, which can be a means of creating shared images or atmospheres for a production of a Shakespeare play.

Forming small groups quickly

- Choose one person to be the leader.
- The other actors move through the space, trying to keep roughly equidistant from one another.
- The leader will clap and say a number. As quickly as possible, all the actors will need to create small groups, in physical contact with one another, of the number chosen. So, if there are fifteen people in the group, and the leader cries out, 'five', then the company will form into five groups of three. This activity is fun and releases tension, but it creates tension too, as part of the game is that the participants should be told that is 'a matter of life and death' (or some such phrase) that they find a group of the right number when the clap happens. The skill is to be dynamic without being flustered.
- Repeat this several times, changing the number called out each time. Sometimes the numbers will not work out and some actors will be left without a group. This can be used, lightly, to encourage a quicker, calmer response from them so that they do get into a group the next time.

Forming a collective shape

- Fill the space by moving through it as before and, as before, one person will clap, to get the ensemble's attention, and then say the name of a shape. It is best to start with a rectangle, as it is the easiest.
- The ensemble must form itself into this shape, as quickly as possible, without verbal or gestural instruction, all arriving at the same time. This is quite challenging and may need to be done several times, as it trains into the group the ability to listen through the body and sense each other in preparation to move and create together.
- Once the rectangle has been created, you can move on to a square. And once that has been mastered, a triangle, which is much more difficult.

This is not easy, but you will bond as an ensemble in failing or as Lecoq says in 'struggle' (2000: 97). Remember that it is not the result that counts here, but the attention you give to one another as you attempt to do it.

Connecting to Shakespeare (shapes)

Now that you are confident in moving swiftly, seamlessly and collectively towards a shared physical and spatial goal, you can move on to creating shapes that will build into a collective, poetic, image memory-bank for the ensemble.

- Move through space as before. This time, after clapping, the leader should call out images from the play that can be formed by the collective bodies of the company. Use the same method of doing it as quickly as possible, with no instructions from anybody within the group of actors, and reaching the shared image, as much as possible, all at the same time.

Here is a list of possible images from *Hamlet*. Adapt this list for the play you are working on.

1. Castle ramparts
2. A vision of a ghost
3. A throne
4. Gothenburg
5. Murdered by poison
6. A grave
7. Drowning.

Each one of these might only take a few seconds to make. Again, to start with, it does not matter what kind of physical shapes you make, as it has more to do with ensemble building and developing the ability to read one another at a physical level, but if you continue to practice this exercise, your group will become so adept that the shapes, or *tableaux* will become more and more useful as potential images for rehearsal and even production purposes.

Connecting to Shakespeare 2 (atmospheres)

In this variation on the exercise, the group will fill the space with an atmosphere appropriate to the play being tackled. This time you are looking for movement and not a collective shape. The company continues to do all these variations together, regardless of which characters they are playing; it is an ensemble exercise. We will use a few suggestions from *Romeo and Juliet*. The prologue from that play gives us many atmospheres to explore. Words suggestive of these atmospheres are marked in bold.

> Two households, both alike in **dignity**,
> In fair Verona, where we lay our scene,
> From ancient **grudge** break to new **mutiny**,
> Where civil blood makes civil hands unclean.
> From forth the fatal loins of these two foes
> A pair of **star-cross'd lovers** take their life,
> Whose misadventured **piteous** overthrows
> Do with their death bury their parents' **strife**.
> The fearful passage of their death-marked love,
> And the **continuance** of their parents' rage,
> Which, but their children's end, nought could remove,
> Is now the two hours' traffic of our stage;
> The which if you with **patient ears** attend,
> What here shall miss, our **toil** shall strive to mend.
>
> (*RJ*, 1.1.1-14)

- While the rest of the group move around the space, one person should read out the words in bold. As each word is read, collectively the ensemble will try to fill the space with the rhythm and energy of whatever each successive word suggests.

- This can be done quickly, just fifteen seconds or so for each word.

Broadly speaking, the group moving and filling the space in response to the word 'dignity' will differ from when the word 'grudge' is mentioned, and the collective movement will be similarly different from these first two when 'mutiny' is mentioned.

- Once you have been through all the words, and notice that something particularly interesting suggests itself in terms of atmosphere, then take it into a collective improvisation towards something more substantial in relation to the story or world or the play.

These very broad brushstrokes will be valuable in seeding the ways in which scenes will be approached. It is useful to have designer and composer involved at this point, as the way in which the company moves, at this stage, will spark ideas for the way to proceed.

Contracting the space

- Continue to move through the space collectively (as instructed on p.37), but this time, the leader will reduce the space that is available to the actors, meaning that everyone will get nearer to one another. Eventually, you will be almost slithering around one another (but not touching). This condition of being tightly packed but still in movement is very dynamic and full of potential.

As you watch or experience this compressed but dynamic human movement, moments, either realistic or more abstract from the plays, can be explored: soldiers in battle, revellers at a party, brawlers in a fight.

Sudden expansion

- Keep this tight-knit movement going for as long as you can stand it, and then, at a signal from the leader, the company will suddenly break up away from each other and rapidly clear the space and stand looking back into it. You will feel an enormous charge in the space. It is the perfect space for an actor to walk into to start speaking.
- Invite one actor to come into the space that is created like this, feel the support that the space gives them, and speak their text.

The space suddenly opening up is potentially very Shakespearean. It is a space where the rich language of Shakespeare is given the chance to breathe. It is the court or the battlefield. This difference between a tightly packed space and a wide-open space is not dissimilar to the two extremes of *éclosion* of Chapter 1. In the world of the physical ensemble, the onus on creating the conditions for the characters, themes and words to emerge most strongly is on the actors. As Lecoq asks at the beginning of the film made about him, *Les Deux Voyages de Jacques Lecoq,* when he demonstrates this sudden expansion of the space with a group of students, '*c'est un bel espace . . . ou est le hero?*' ('it's a beautiful space . . . where is the hero?') (1998). Whether it is Hamlet, Cleopatra or Dogberry from *Much Ado About Nothing,* the ensemble creates the space for them to speak. They are all heroes in this context.

Making it physical

Shakespeare's plays are very physical. The way in which the plays are written, with long complex thoughts, is physically demanding for actors. Shakespeare's world is physical too – full of dance, fighting, singing. A group of actors embarking on a Shakespearean journey will benefit from being physically robust.

Lecoq's pedagogy never advocates fitness for fitness's sake, but as Lecoq himself explains in *The Moving Body*, he returned to his roots in physical education and the re-education of the war-wounded, in his teaching: 'When I started, I used George Hébert's "natural method" which analyses movement under eleven categories: pushing, pulling, climbing, walking, running, jumping, lifting, carrying, attacking, defending, swimming. [. . .] The analysis of a physical action does not mean expressing an opinion but acquiring physical awareness which will form an indispensable basis for acting' (2000: 72). Shakespeare's plays, are, of course, not unique in their physical demands but many of the most successful ensembles who approach Shakespeare will take time to ensure that the company does extensive physical preparation.

Running

- Assemble the company at one side of the rehearsal space in a clump. At a signal from the director or teacher, the group will run as fast as possible to the other side of the room. Once the clump has reached the other side, the company

turns as quickly as possible and then feels the rush of air that will suddenly hit them.
- Do it again, as not everyone will feel it forcefully the first time.

As soon as you have done this, the company will get a glimpse of their own collective power. There is something about the vacuum that is created by the speed of running together and then the wave of air that hits the group that is very compelling. In their production of *The Winter's Tale,* Complicité prepared for the devising of the mysterious transformation of Hermione's 'statue' in the fifth act by running collectively around the 'huge rehearsal space, for about ten minutes until we could not bear it any more' (Arden, 2021). The company had been building up to this climax and wanted to feel as if 'it [Hermione's transformation] was really happening' (Arden, 2021). The brute physical force of the ensemble running together helped them to realize the potential of this moment. Theatre du Soleil's iconic opening of their *Richard II* featured the actors running on in a long line around vast stage to the beat of loud Japanese-style drum music, stopping abruptly one after the other and collapsing to the ground. It was an extraordinary evocation of the medieval court of Richard 'transposed' via a playfulness and physicality, directed by Arianne Mnouchkine, who studied with Lecoq, as did the core members of the company. Running, in both these instances, was transposed into something tellingly poetic.

Along with purely athletic exercises, Lecoq was pretty dismissive of 'exercises in group dynamics – e.g. holding hands before beginning a performance – they are very nice and helpful for the group but not for professional actors' (2000: 70). Lecoq's idea of building ensemble was to get his students to team up on a weekly basis and 'struggle' in the devising process known as *auto-cours*. He asserted that 'The only internal harmony that matters' in comparison to 'gymnastic methods which I call comforting' is 'that of play' (2000: 70). It is very useful for an ensemble to learn to play together by using simple, often children's, games.

Ball games

Ball games do not feature in Lecoq's training but play a large part in the ensemble building work of Complicité and other companies.

- You will need a ball. A light ball for playing with at the beach is best. If you do not have a ball, then some clothes, wrapped up together, will do.

- First, get the group into a circle and practice keeping the ball in the air between you for as long as possible. You can use anything – hands, head or feet – but the easiest and most reliable way to keep the ball in the air is to pat it up with open palms.

- Then set the whole group (or split into smaller teams) the task of moving from one part of the space to another while passing the ball between the actors in the patting it up way we have just described.

- The group (or groups) then must move as quickly as possible as a team from one side of the room to the other making sure that everyone has touched the ball at least once. If you have two or more groups, you can make this into a race.

- To vary this, and raise the stakes, incorporate some of George Hébert's eleven key movement activities (**climbing, jumping, carrying**) into the collective travelling and passing of the ball:

  1. Place a chair or table in the space and make sure that everybody **climbs** on and over it.
  2. Create another obstacle over which the whole group must **jump**.
  3. Make it a condition that every member must be **carried** by one or more of the rest of the group during the exercise.

Catherine Alexander, a long-time Complicité collaborator and actor trainer, thinks that one of the most important advantages of a Lecoq training is that it trains actors to think more in multiple spatial planes, as these complex ball games promote. She argues that the predominant model in traditional actor training posits the space between two actors as the most important one, the one that is talked across, whereas the Lecoq pedagogy promotes the story-telling connection to the space all around the actor as the most important one (Alexander, 2022).

Connecting to Shakespeare (improvisation)

Part of the success of director Phyllida Lloyd's ensemble building on the all-female Donmar Trilogy of *Julius Caesar, Henry IV* and *The Tempest* was that 'we always improvised' (Lloyd, 2022).1 Even though they had the Shakespearean text, the company spent weeks or months improvising their way into the means of making the production work in response to the people, the times and the conditions of the production. Lloyd talks of improvising around the themes of the plays. This involved actors playing outside of the actual text, or imagining ways in which characters might interact. With the whole trilogy of plays, her concerns were themes like:

> the individual in relation to the group. The individual in relation to parliament, the king in relation to the army, the person who has just landed on a desert island in relation to the islanders who have been there for an eternity.

In an improvisation for *Henry IV*, Lloyd talks of playing with a moment when Prince Hal 'has taken a lot of drugs and a pint of lager', the army is 'in repose, on guard', and the King, Hal's father, has 'just read the *Daily Mail*, and seen that Hal has been wearing a Nazi uniform at a stag night' (redolent, in part, of the UK's contemporary royal family) and is in a high state of tension and very irritated (Lloyd, 2022). The improvisations use contemporary references and contemporary language to let the ensemble explore the plays somewhat on their own terms.

- Take a scene from the play you are working on and play it out in really simple terms.
- Use your own modern language for the improvisation.

---

[1]Phyllida Lloyd's Donmar Trilogy began at the Donmar Warehouse in 2012 with a production of *Julius Caesar* set in a women's prison. This was followed in 2014 by *Henry IV* at the Donmar Warehouse and 2016 by *The Tempest* at the Donmar King's Cross, both using the same prison setting.

- Allow the events of the scene to unfold more quickly than they would if you were saying all of the lines. You are creating an alternative to the scene which will then feed the way in which the text is acted.

An improvisation on a Shakespeare scene will often be sourced from something that feels adjacent to the actual scene, and may sometimes be contradictory. Simon McBurney, artistic director of Complicité, talks of how they happened upon the energy and style for the prison scene in act 4 of their production of *Measure for Measure* by improvising around the scene as if it were a farce, 'with lots of doors banging' (McBurney, 2022). That game, with 'doors banging', became the guiding force for treating this seemingly sad scene with a comic energy, creating an atmosphere suitable for this tragi-comic play.

Here are some really simple improvisation strategies that may release something in a scene:

1. Everybody is laughing all the way through the scene.
2. Each character imagines listening to different kind of music as they improvise the scene.
3. Imagine the scene in an inappropriate genre: quick-fire comedy for a serious scene, grand operatic tragedy for a funny scene, mumble-core for a romantic scene.

Passing a clap

This next exercise creates a physicalized dynamic reality of connection between the company members which is then taken into an exploration of scene playing.

- Form a circle and each clap once going round the circle.
- Allow space between each clap to get shorter and shorter.
- Encourage the clap to be 'passed' from one person to the next.
- Encourage the clap to go around as fast as it possibly can.
- Get the entire group to 'watch' the clap as it whizzes around the circle. Keep going as long as you can until it breaks down or the leader stops the game.

This game will create a real sense of excitement and a shared vision (of the clap as ball or object being passed). It is a clear embodied metaphor for how the whole company takes responsibility for the imaginary world of the play because for the illusion to work the whole group must partake in the collective sensing and seeing of the clap, or 'ball' being passed around.

- Re-start the passing of a clap, but this time it is passed across the space from person to person. Imagine that the clap is like throwing a ball. You pass the ball with a particular energy. The clap might be quick, sharp and seem to travel across the space very quickly. Alternatively, the clap could be a kind of lazy, comfortable clap that seems to loop through the air. The person who is 'catching' the clap tries to catch it with an energy similar to that with which it has been thrown. The catch is also a clap of the hands. Each exchange, therefore, contains two claps.

- Pass the clap in this way across the circle a few times. Then create some variety by passing it to the person right beside you or by pretending to bounce the 'ball' on the floor between you and another person. Be as inventive as you like. The object of the game is for the catcher to be in sympathy with the way the clap is passed and for the whole ensemble to share in a vision of what is occurring.

- Continue to play the game in this way but now with everyone moving around the space. There will be long looping passes from one side of the room to the other and short intimate passes to a person right next to you and everything else between.

- The leader can add more claps in as you go to make it more challenging. As ever, the ability for the group to sustain more complex tasks with calmness and resolve will greatly strengthen the ensemble's ability to create collectively.

Connecting to Shakespeare (speaking and listening)

This is an energy and vocal exercise which builds on the **fishing net** in Chapter 1 and the clapping exercise we have just described. Each actor will need to know a short speech from the play, and the better you know it the more useful the exercise will be.

- Split into pairs. One actor will speak the lines and the other will guide the way in which they are delivered.
- Before any words are said, you will prepare the space between you physically by passing the clap between you as detailed in the previous exercise.
- Establish a nice comfortable rhythm between you, to start with, like a knock-up, in tennis.
- Once you are comfortable, find as much variety as you can in the clap that you pass and be particularly attentive to how you catch what is being thrown at you.
- As you pass the clap see if you can make the person who is catching extend themselves. Pass it to them so they have to reach up, reach down and reach to either side. Vary the speed, direction and quality of the passes.

Now explore the text with the clapping. The objective here is to connect the two actors via the text in a way that is embodied, palpable and unpredictable. Throughout the exercise, actor B leads actor A's delivery. Actor B passes a clap to A. A receives it and passes a clap to B with the same energy and intention as the clap that they received, while speaking a line of text.

> CASSIUS
> Why, man, he doth bestride the narrow world
> Like a colossus, and we petty men
> Walk under his huge legs and peep about
> To find ourselves dishonorable graves.
> Men at some time are masters of their fates.
> The fault, dear Brutus, is not in our stars
> But in ourselves, that we are underlings.
>
> (*JC*, 1.2.134-140)

- Actor A is speaking Cassius' lines.
- B passes a clap to A. A receives it with a matching energy.
- A keeps this energy and passes a clap to B while saying – 'Why man he doth bestride the narrow world'. B receives the clap.

- B passes a clap with a new type of energy to A. A receives it with a matching energy.
- A keeps this energy and passes a clap to B while saying – 'Like a Colossus and we petty men'. B receives the clap.
- B passes a clap with a new type of energy to A. A receives it with a matching energy.
- A keeps this energy and passes a clap to B while saying – 'Walk under his huge legs and peep about'. B receives the clap.
- B passes a clap with a new type of energy to A. A receives it with a matching energy.
- A keeps this energy and passes a clap to B while saying – 'To find ourselves dishonourable graves'. B receives the clap.

Etc.

- Try one version of the exercise, for example with a low slow clap, followed by a high arching clap, followed by a clap bounced off the wall, followed by a sharp, zingy clap.
- Try another version of the exercise, with the claps in a different order, for example a high arching clap, followed by a sharp, zingy clap, followed by a low slow clap, followed by a clap bounced off the wall.
- Immediately after doing this last version, actor A should speak the lines without clapping, retaining a sense of the energy and intention of the claps, but with both actors standing still.

You can watch an example of this exercise using Video 3: https://bloomsbury.pub/shakespeare-and-lecoq

This is a good way to make sure, at a fundamental level, that the lines that Shakespeare has written become interwoven between the actors, and that the impulses are embedded physically. Simon McBurney, in discussing Leontes' journey in *The Winter's Tale*, talks of how 'the impulses of the body lead to his tyranny and that tyranny begins in his body'. He speaks, similarly, of *Macbeth* containing a 'paradox or painful joke', because

Macbeth is a man so aware of his own world and so alive to his body, and so conscious that he can really feel the consequence of what he is doing. The terrible thing is how conscious Macbeth is of his own mind, through the most sublime poetry, which is, in turn, deeply embodied. (McBurney, 2022)

Productions of Shakespeare that have a Lecoq influence are likely to abound with physicality. Complicité and Théâtre du Soleil's inevitable physicality has already been mentioned. Cheek by Jowl, who have often had Lecoq-trained movement director, Jane Gibson, working on their shows, always begin their Shakespeare production processes with movement. The Royal Shakespeare Company has had Lecoq-trained movement directors, notably Ayse Tashkiran and Sue Lefton (who was also 'Master of Dance' on *Hamlet* at Shakespeare's Globe in 2000) to bind the company through physicality. Some touring companies take things even further in that the physical games and/or work goes beyond the stage and rehearsal room. Footsbarn Travelling Theatre, a company whose work 'emerg[es] out of the Lecoq tradition' (Tunstall, 2016: 269) have created an extraordinary body of Shakespeare productions partly out of a collective living arrangement on one hand and in the hard graft of erecting and dismantling their circus tent together whenever they travel to perform. On a much smaller scale, The Handlebards do outdoor Shakespeare in a Lecoq-style way, with the four performers cycling from venue to venue with all of their set and costumes with them on the bikes, creating the conditions for great physical fitness and camaraderie along the way. Artistic director Tom Dixon says of their working methods: 'If you are active in the day and exposed to the sun or rain, actors seem to become much more alive, physically tired but mentally awake, and at those moments, it becomes difficult to put up a façade and we are most open' (Dixon, 2022).

Exploring the play as an ensemble

Basic group movement like a shoal of fish

  a. **In a triangle**
- Clump together in the middle of the space with a few feet in between each of you and then spread out into something of a triangle. There will be one person at each of the three apexes of the triangle.
- Invite one of them to move forwards. They are, for the moment, the leader.

- The others will follow them until the leader reaches the edge of the space and can go no further, at which point they turn around or swivel. The group follows suit and turns so that one of the other two at corners will be at the front.
- They then start to move forward and everyone else follows them.
- Do this several times across the space. It may be a bit mechanical to start while you get the hang of it. Keep to the three leaders as you get to feel how this works.

b. **Changes of speed**

- Carry on as above but now each time one of the three leaders takes over, they will walk forward at a different speed.
- Each new leader can make more radical shifts in speed, like running, jogging, dawdling and even crawling.

c. **Shoaling in an unspecified shape**

- When the whole group has got the idea, then loosen it up, so it is no longer a triangle but more of an unspecific shape. Now there are no designated leaders and so someone must take the initiative to move in a particular way each time there is a change of direction.
- When the leader reaches the edge of the space, they will turn, and depending on how far they turn, a new person from somewhere at the side or back of the group will take over as leader.

There will be some grey areas where not everyone knows what is going on, but that is half the point; to stay calm, open, playful and connected to the other actors without being directly instructed. The leader might also decide to turn before they get to the edge of the space to make it more unpredictable.

- Introduce the same variations in speed described earlier for the triangle – running, joggling, dawdling, crawling and so on.

d. **Moving in different rhythms**

- Each person who takes over as leader will start to move off with a different rhythm. By different rhythm, we mean something distinct from speed or tempo. As you set off with a particular rhythm, it might also contain a feeling like being in a hurry, being languid, fraught or happy.

e. **Moving as animals**

- As you get better at this game, you can add any inspiration you want as the leader. Animals are a good place to start. Each new leader offers a different animal: birds in one direction, primates in another direction and so on. Don't feel you need to be particularly accurate to the animal but take on their rhythm. Every time the shoal changes direction there will be a new leader at the front.

As you get more used to doing this, the distinction between who is leading and who is following becomes less, and it feels like the whole group makes each of the decisions, more like a shoal of fish moving together on deep instinct.

f. **Connecting to Shakespeare (ensemble character exploration)**

Continue the pattern of moving through the space in a shoal-like way, but this time instead of animals, be characters from the play.

- Form a large, loose clump, as before, and each person who takes the lead will move as the character or one of the characters they are playing.
- Once you have done this for as long as feels interesting, make it that each person who leads will lead with a character they are not playing. This stretches the collective imagination of the ensemble. It does not matter if you do a good impression of another character or not. The focus is, as in most parts of this chapter, about extending the group's ability to work together and make mistakes together.

g. **Adding sound**

- Continue this exercise but add sound. Go through both of the steps: leading as your own character and then leading as somebody else's character. Allow the sounds to be very free and almost abstract.

If you are working on *As You Like It*, it might be that you play a version of this where you make sounds (a) for your own character when you take the lead, and having played that switch to (b) creating a sound world along with the movement for another character in the play when you lead. For example:

a. The first actor (who is cast as Phoebe) moves across the stage making sarcastic sounds and movement, as sarcasm is one of her traits, with the rest of the company following suit. She turns, and the actor playing Duke Senior takes over the lead and moves, making welcoming sounds, as this is part of his character. This continues until you have had all the actors explore at least one character.

b. The first actor to lead might be cast as Rosalind, but instead moves and makes sounds that they think Touchstone might make and sounds and movements that they think represents him in some way – these might be comical, free sounds, since Touchstone is a fool. When they turn, the actor cast as Charles the Wrestler takes over and moves and makes sound which are connected in some way to Celia (maybe *teasing* sounds as one of the characteristics of Celia is to tease Rosalind). Keep going until everyone has had a few goes.

This is a great way to encourage the whole company to take some ownership of all the characters in the play. We have made some suggestions here, as to how to use this shoaling exercise but, of course, once you have understood the principle of it then you can adapt it to your own needs. Lecoq graduate, Briony O'Callaghan, from Flabbergast Theatre, talks of using this exercise for 'hours on end' in preparation for their recent production of *Macbeth*, to 'develop the physical listening to one another' (O'Callaghan, 2022).

When actors, designers, composers and directors find an ensemble language to explore with over time, then there is more opportunity to make powerful discoveries about the nature of the work itself and to make powerful connections between the time and culture for which Shakespeare wrote the plays and the time and culture for which they are being produced.

3

Exploring the story

Shakespeare took most of his stories from pre-existing sources. His great skill, therefore, was not in the invention, but in the *telling* of the stories by an almost inexhaustible variety of characters. Lecoq's pedagogy is also concerned with story-telling. Every week, when the students present work in front of the teachers and rest of the school, the pieces always require a sense of narrative. The piecing together of events in a satisfying way is one of the focuses of the training. In this chapter, on story, we will focus on how Lecoq's methods can help to bring out the structure of the story of a Shakespeare play, and how gesture can be used to create visual structure within a single scene. Fundamental to our approach here is that Shakespeare, as a playwright, offered his players great freedom with how to stage his plays, by imposing very few stage directions. The stage of the Globe Theatre, for which he wrote many of his plays, would have been largely bare, with little scenery. This allowed for a quick, almost film-like cutting between scenes. Late into the twentieth and on into our own century, Lecoq's school still favoured the bare boards of its *Grande Salle* (Big Hall) with the minimum technical electrical resources, and only then, when sharing with the public. Stories are conjured with the sparest of means through the actors' bodies. If Shakespeare's skill was in weaving tapestries of language to send the audience into imagined realms, then Lecoq's students come out of the school equipped with their bodies trained to create shapes and rhythms in space to explore the story.

Story as a kinetic structure

As discussed in the Introduction to the book, part of each day at the Lecoq school is given over to *auto-cours*. The students are given a theme connected to the work taking place in movement and improvisation classes at the time: 'A Place and an Event', 'The Exodus', 'The Fight' etc and must fashion a piece of their own, attempting to incorporate whatever it is they are learning in class at the time. In the second year, the most successful of these pieces are gathered and presented to an invited public audience in a '*Soirée*'.

For many years the very first *auto-cours* title given to students has been '*Un lieu et un évènement*' (A place and an event). The point of the theme is that there is somewhere, and in that somewhere, something happens. Lecoq clearly foregrounds story at the beginning of the journey at the school.

Critical discussions of Shakespeare's work often focus on language, theme and context. However, an exploration of story which is clear, felt and embodied is also extremely helpful for a company beginning to create a new production of one of these plays. Asking the question: 'What happens?' in the play is a very powerful one. Solving the issue of 'what happens' as opposed to 'how we do it' is a key difference when considering a new production. We can argue that the former is audience-related and the latter company-related. One of Lecoq's overriding concerns, which sets the pedagogy apart from conventional actor training, is the consideration of the audience. Nearly every exercise at the *Ecole Jacques Lecoq* puts the audience first. Indeed, in the classroom, when critiquing students' work, Lecoq would often look around at the other students near him to gather consensus, as if to say that his word was not enough but needed to be corroborated by the audience.

In *The Moving Body* Lecoq stresses the importance of giving pleasure to an audience, as well as to oneself:

Unfortunately, many people enjoy expressing themselves . . . and forgetting that they must not be the only ones to get pleasure from it: spectators must receive pleasure, too. There are many teachers who confuse these two points of view. The difference between the act of expression and the act of creation is this: in the act of expression one plays for oneself alone rather than for any spectators. I always look for an actor who 'shines', who develops a space around himself in which the spectators are also present. (2000: 16–17)

When Complicité produced their version of *The Winter's Tale* in 1992, they applied themselves to the story in a concrete and ensemble way. Among other things, they asked themselves what the eight or nine key events are and then proceeded to explore those with drawings, gestures and play, until they reached some kind of 'scaffolding' to underpin the 'kinetic reality' of the story. (Arden, 2021)

Ten key moments from the play

- Think about the play you are working on. What happens in it?
- Write down the ten key things that happen in it.

Here is an example for *Macbeth:*

1. Some witches tell Macbeth he is going to be king and his friend Banquo's sons will be king.

2. Macbeth tells his wife about the prophecy.

3. She persuades him to kill the current king who is staying with them.

4. He kills the king.

5. He also has his friend Banquo killed.

6. The witches tell Macbeth to 'Beware Macduff'.

7. Macbeth has Macduff's family killed.

8. Macbeth's wife goes mad and dies.

9. Macduff and Malcolm (the old king's son) bring an army to fight against Macbeth.

10. Macbeth is killed and Malcolm takes the crown.

It does not need to be 'right', and it is available to be revised, maybe repeatedly as you devise your production.

Drawings

- Once you have made these preliminary stabs at what the story seems to be, then make a drawing of each of them. The drawings can obviously be of any quality and realistic or abstract. The key is to get some images of what the story contains. Put the drawings on the wall, discuss them and let them bleed their way into your collective thinking.

Soundscapes

- Split the group into two.
- Make it a kind of *auto-cours*. Invite one actor from each group to be a kind of conductor. Be prepared to share the work with the rest of the company after an agreed amount of time.
- Ask each group to make a soundscape for each of the moments you have chosen. You can start by just using open sound – the vowels A, E, I, O, U. You will be surprised, once you simply set to the task of creating sounds for different moments, at how different they can be.
- Depending on the company, you can move on to create soundscapes with whatever you have to hand. Other non-vowel sounds are useful in moderation, for example, more percussive consonant-type sounds. Hisses, clicks and pops using your vocal apparatus can be mixed in with more open sounds.

You do not have to be experts to get something out of it. The different soundscapes create different emotional landscapes for the actors and company to feed off. And of course, the sounds may lead on to decisions about how the music and 'soundtrack' of the production will develop.

- Finally, do some soundscapes for each of your chosen moments with any instruments you have in the rehearsal space and also with any objects you have to hand.

The story points in gesture

- Divide the group into two halves and have each group concoct a gestural version of each of these preliminary ten story points. Use your bodies in the space to offer up embodied sketches of each story beat from one to ten. These are more like tableaux or snapshots of the story, but there might be some movement into, and out of, each tableau.

- Use twenty or so minutes to make your snapshots and then share with the rest of the company. Compare the versions and take what you have discovered on into how you want to tell the story.

Mostly, the work we propose on story is designed to further the ensemble's embodiment of the play. It is not enough for an actor just to embody their part. The Lecoq training instils the notion, in the students, from beginning to end, that they are part of a greater entity. The training encourages students to feel that they are part of an endlessly moving, and suggestive space. Catherine Alexander, founder of the Collaborative and Devised Theatre course at the Royal Central School of Speech and Drama and a long-term collaborator with Complicité, has said, 'In order for an ensemble to communicate a story effectively they must develop a shared understanding of the story and the languages needed to tell it. When this deep preparation has happened, the creative work is richer' (Alexander, 2018).

Exploring the story of the whole play in mime

Children gain their understanding of the world around them by miming. They mimic what they see and hear. They replay with their whole body those aspects of life in which they will be called to on to participate. In this way they learn about life and little by little, take possession of it. (Lecoq, 2006: 1)

In this exercise we suggest how the ensemble can use mime or gesture to learn about the story that they are engaging in. Through whole body movements, the company familiarizes itself with the heart of the story.

Mime the whole play

- Divide the company into pairs. Spread yourselves around the room.

- With whatever level of knowledge of the story that the pair of actors have, one actor should play out a version of the story to the other actor using mime, movement and gesture only.
- The miming actor can impersonate characters, play multiple characters and embody settings, objects and relationships. See if things visible and invisible can be mimed or conjured with gestures.
- You have ten minutes to do it. Depending on the size of the company there may be several improvisations going on at once.

To make it possible for various pairs to be doing this simultaneously, it is best that it be done without words or even sound. But the actors who are miming the story should feel free to move around the space if they need to. This might generate a slight atmosphere of anarchy which is, we hope, creative. The students at the Lecoq school have to conjure different worlds and stories each week in their *auto-cours* groups, working cheek by jowl with all the other groups, in various different spoken languages and so a faint whiff of gleeful chaos often accompanies Lecoq-influenced creatives as they travel on into the world.

It is vital that the actors miming do not rush. They might know the story very well or scarcely at all. Both levels of knowledge can produce fascinating results. Keep it intimate, with one actor sharing moments from the story with the other. There should be no hurry. There is no pressure to impress anyone. It is important to emphasize this so people relax as much as possible.

Some actors will get no further than Act 1. Some might deliver a version of the whole story. It is important, here, to realize that mistakes can be very valuable, even more valuable often than getting it right:

> Error is not just acceptable, it is necessary for the continuation of life, provided it is not too great. A large error is a catastrophe; a small error is essential for the enhancing existence. (Lecoq, 2000: 21)

Annabel Arden, founder member of Complicité, talks of harvesting 'propositions' or proposals from the actors at the early part of the process (Arden, 2022). As the actor muddles their way through a mimed version of as much of the story as they can remember, their own interests and strengths will come to the surface, and these details may go on to provide vital clues as to how to retell the story in the best way for the company in hand. The fact that it is very difficult or impossible for one actor to tell the whole story in ten minutes is part of the exercise's power. Its virtual impossibility will, hopefully, release the actor into not caring too much if they do it well or not and consequently their sense of play will come to the fore. Every actor's 'proposition' or proposal will be utterly different, and this helps to make the ensemble production a direct result of what the actual members of the company bring to the process at that moment in time. Simon McBurney explains that in preparing *Winter's Tale* everything was happening 'within a social and political context – then and there – and there are ways of talking about your time, and body, and nature, which link it to an absolute immediate moment' and that was what gave that production its 'driving sense of the urgency' (2022).

Continue to mime the whole play

- Within the pairs, the actor who is watching must be watching carefully. This is as important a role as the miming. In any ensemble process, the quality of the company is determined by how the actors support one another. Lecoq describes his school as 'an education in seeing' (2000: 20).

- When the first actor's ten minutes is up, the pairs of actors can confer over what has just happened. A feature of Lecoq's pedagogy is an avoidance of intellectualizing and an insistence on finding play, so let the initial conversation be along the lines of the watcher saying, 'I liked it when . . .' 'you moved me when . . .' and 'it made me laugh when . . .' and so on, with a view to collaborating, in play, for the next stage of the exercise.

- Repeat the process but with the roles reversed.

- When the second actor has shared their mimed version of the story, the two actors will join forces for an *auto-cours*.

- The two actors decide on ten moments, chosen from both of their improvisations and prepare them to share with the rest of the group.

- Take twenty minutes to prepare this before you share it. The timings here are only suggestions, but keeping it brisk creates a kind of freshness to the work.

- Once all the versions have been watched and commented on, it would be good moment to have a general discussion about how the play's story can be best told.

Exploring sections of the story

How does the story move?

Actor, Toby Jones, who trained with Lecoq, remembers that when collaborating with Complicité on *Measure for Measure*, the question that was repeatedly asked was 'how does the story move?' (Jones, 2022). Annabel Arden, who directed *The Winter's Tale* for Complicité, talks fondly of how, when approaching a Shakespeare play with a company whose skill did not naturally lie in verse-speaking and who were not all even English speakers, it was vital to find 'another route into the story' (Arden, 2022). They, therefore, worked out the story in a series of *auto-cours*. With limited means and limited props or scenery, they returned to the thing they knew best: movement. They recognized that the most powerful way to advance the story was to improvise with how the spaces changed. The *where* keeps changing, and who is in the *where* changes too. That became the task: 'to divide the company and to explore, with bodies in space, before even portraying character or delivering text. The structure of what happens was worked out dynamically in shorthand [. . .] by the whole company' (Arden, 2022). As Arden explains: 'as we were not used to sitting around and being told what to do by a director it was always more productive to split the company into two groups' (Arden, 2022) and to devise, with mainly just bodies and movement, but also the odd prop or bit of furniture that happened to be in the rehearsal room.

With *The Winter's Tale*, the company was interested in the customs of the play's world, the structures of lawgiving and hospitality and the patterns that abound in the play, about which, as Arden explains, they could have been 'very intellectual', but they chose not to be. Instead, they asked physical, practical questions like, 'What does it mean to walk in a circle? How does one space change from one thing into another?' (Arden, 2022). The small devising groups were tasked, then, to get from one bit of the story to another without worrying 'about getting all the text in . . . or . . . about playing all the characters' (Arden, 2022). Arden recalls vividly a part of the rehearsal process, where they had to

> take a scene or a group of scenes and it was clear that the story had to move forward, and it had to be exciting. And so, space had to change, and people had to change and clearly something had to develop. That in itself was the challenge: How can we move from one situation to the next? How are we going to do it? If it has to go from a small room where someone who is essentially a servant confronts a powerful person and gets overruled, to a completely different space which is populated by children to yet another space where two people you have not seen before (or not for a long while) are encountering a spiritual force. (Arden, 2022)

Arden is describing, here, a version of a narrative progression in *The Winter's Tale* (2.3). It is very broad and gives a strong indication of how Lecoq's interest in dynamics is at play. The language she uses is archetypal rather than specific. She does not use the character names as this is not as important as the essence of what is going on. It is, to borrow, an expression from music, like laying down a baseline. The company devised a dynamic thread for how that particular group could get from one part of the story to another without consideration for who is playing who, what the text will sound like, or the details of the play. The forward propulsion of the story is what matters, and, in this example, this is done by foregrounding the transformations of the space. The origins of this kind of approach can be traced back to the Lecoq school where many of the company of *The Winter's Tale* had studied. Lecoq describes an exercise in the form of an *auto-cours* where the students are asked to retell the story of a well-known film in gesture:

> I ask the students to recreate a whole film without words, using only gestures. Cartoon mime can make use of any cinematic technique: close-ups, long-shots, illusions, flashbacks, in short, the whole repertoire of the modern language of moving pictures, with its rhythms, its brilliance, its ellipses, all transposed into the dimension of theatre. (Lecoq, 2000: 109)

We suggest allowing yourself the freedom of this kind of cinematic bending of space and time to approach the next exercise.

Devising the movement through the story

- Split the group into two so that each group will have an audience for the work. If you are a large group then it may be worth splitting into three or four groups.
- Each group will spend an allotted amount of time working through a section of the story, primarily in terms of how the space changes from scene to scene or even moment to moment.

Imagine you are working on *Twelfth Night*. You are in a group of five. Your task is to improvise your way through the first three scenes or so, of the play. Your emphasis is on the story. You have a bench, some coats and a ball in the rehearsal room. You have twenty minutes to come up with something. So, if the changing spaces exercise in Chapter 2 was improvising, this is improvising and devising. 'Devising' in this context, and in the abovementioned examples with soundscapes and the mimed story exercise, is where improvisations are done, discussed, re-done and then presented to others. There are, of course, an infinite number of ways this could be done and so these are simply suggestions to give you a lead:

- In each group, describe the story to yourselves in its essence and then confirm that that is what you will focus on.
- Decide on what kind of spaces there are and who is in them and, broadly, what they are doing.
- Play out in very broad strokes what you have decided on and then review and refine.
- Show it to the rest of the company.

Be mindful that, at this stage, you are not responsible for solving how the story gets transmitted and it might be that just one little detail of what you do catches the attention of the ensemble and then that is used going forward in the rehearsal process. We are going to give you the very barest version of what the first three scenes of

Twelfth Night could be like in terms of moving through the spaces in a similar way to what Complicité did with *Winter's Tale.*

1. There is a confined space where a rich man is moping about love to his servants.

2. This changes into a wide, wild space into which lands a desperate young woman who makes a deal with a man.

3. This changes into an interior space where a woman harangues a man. He defends himself and welcomes his friend with whom he plots and dances.

As you can see, this is a version of the essence of the story of this part of the story. It is an attempt to summon the bare-bones and it is scant on names or details as, at this stage as we want you to focus on the underlying movement of the story, via the spaces that it inhabits, before you get involved with specifics.

Now imagine that your group has to improvise and devise the through-movement of this part of the story. Other groups could be working on other parts of the story. It might end up with something a bit like this. You are not trying to solve the staging but use what you have: bodies, space, movement and a few simple props to make some 'propositions' (Arden, 2022) or proposals.

1. In the first section, the rich man (he's a Duke and so we are making that assumption) may be lying on a bench, idly playing with the ball. He offers a coat to the servant whom he needs to go to his beloved.

2. In the second section, the bench becomes debris from the shipwreck the young woman has escaped. The ball is a reminder of the brother she has lost. A coat is offered as a disguise the young woman will adopt.

3. In the third section, a coat is taken off as the man is coming in from outside after probably drinking. The bench might be offered by the woman as a refuge for the drunk man to sit on. The ball is kicked and miraculously caught by the other man who is not as quick-witted as the first but is happy to play along with the man who drinks.

    • Now you have a quick version of the very barest of bones of the events of the story you must figure out how it is that you get from one to the other. How does scenario (1) turn into (2) and how might (2) morph into (3)? They are not just scene changes. The dynamics of those transitions from one space to another will give you great clues as to how the story moves.

This is, of course, a naïve way to describe the first part of *Twelfth Night*. We could (as could have Arden's company with *The Winter's Tale*) have intellectualized about it, but choose, purposefully, to recast the story in this light. It becomes, now, an essence of the story, using whatever happens to be in the space, acted out by actors who may or may not be playing the characters mentioned. Now you have imagined this process with us, you are ready to redeploy the method on the play that you are preparing. We are aware that the three sections we have chosen coincide with three scenes, and they happen to be quite short scenes. Sometimes in longer scenes, the dramatic 'space' and characters in it will change more, so choose the amount of story that you feel that each group cope with in the amount of time that you allot.

Exploring the story of a scene

This exercise introduces the important notion of *'attitudes'*. The exercise starts to address how individual actors can take responsibility for letting the story live with clarity in their bodies.

'Attitude' is a key word in the Lecoq pedagogy, and it does not have a very satisfactory translation into English. The English word 'attitude' suggests a kind of opinion which is not useful. Lecoq asserts – 'I use the word attitude to convey a powerful moment of stasis, isolated within a movement' (2000: 81). Essentially you will be producing tableaux – still, silent images of moments from a scene.

- Read the scene, and decide among you, what are the key story moments in the scene. Here is an example from Act 3 Scene 4 of *King Lear*. You can, of course, transfer this exercise to a scene that you are working on.

1. Kent leads Lear to a hovel.
2. Lear thinks about 'poor naked wretches' (3.4.28).

3. The Fool appears scared.
4. Edgar appears, wild, as Poor Tom.
5. Lear is intrigued by Poor Tom.
6. Lear takes his clothes off to be like him.
7. Gloucester finds them all.
8. He implores Lear to go inside.
9. Lear agrees.
10. Lear encourages his 'philosopher' (3.4.150), Poor Tom, to come too.

- Create a tableau for each of the chosen moments.

  - Be obvious. Make gestures that feel like you are explaining things.
  - Use your whole body.
  - Use your arms to point and indicate.
  - Use different levels in space, lying right down on the ground, kneeling up, sitting down, standing and any number of different angles and *attitudes* in standing.
  - Think about the distance between yourselves. Even changing that distance can have a big impact.
  - If you have decided on how you will be playing to the audience (in-the-round, traverse, straight on etc.) then proximity to them will also inform how you place yourselves in the tableaux.

- Next, run the tableaux together one after the other. What kind of rhythm imposes itself as you go from one to another? What kind of spaces open up? In this instance, 'space' means the shapes that the bodies make, how they seem to resonate outwards and what kind of meaning or emotion is suggested by them.

- A final exploration of this story-telling exercise is to play the scene with the text without any pre-arranged tableaux, but notice which of the tableaux want to impose themselves in the acting of the scene. Notice, too, what new *attitudes* are emerging in your individual and collective playing.

You are developing the skill of letting yourself be aware of the stories that your bodies can tell before the words even emerge. Simon McBurney still likes to use Lecoq's French expression, '*le geste en-dessous*' ('the gesture underneath' or 'the gesture that supports') to describe the way in which this kind of embodied method can cement a sense of the 'rhythms' and 'architecture' and of the play for the company and audience (McBurney, 2022).

4

Exploring the world of the play

The world of the play is more than where the story is set. It is more than the conceit of the director. In ensemble productions, the world of the play will emerge through weeks of improvisation and experimentation. It is a collaboration between director, actors, designer and composer. This takes time and often it is best accomplished by groups who have worked together often, so that much of the theatrical language used within the company is shared. Théâtre du Soleil, a company who feature throughout this book, created, collectively, memorable landscapes for their Shakespearean trilogy of *Richard II, Twelfth Night* and *Henry IV,* fusing East and South Asian forms with their own methods of improvising, and collaborating. Footsbarn Travelling Theatre has created many playful productions of Shakespeare's plays, blending folk traditions, puppetry, masks and irreverence to create a particular world. Complicité's Shakespeare worlds in their *Winter's Tale* and *Measure for Measure* emerged partly from games and objects that were in the rehearsal room (Arden, 2021). Complicité founder member Annabel Arden uses the expression 'poetic matrix', which was coined by Annie Castledine, a co-director on *The Winter's Tale* (Arden, 2022) to describe the way in which they go about constructing the world of a play. The same expression could easily be applied to the other Lecoq-inspired companies mentioned in this book, who are fusing space, improvisation and movement, with rhythms, words and music, to create complex poetic spaces designed to linger long afterwards in the spectator's mind.

In this chapter we will lead you through some of Lecoq's exercises from near the beginning of the 'journey', as Lecoq liked to call it (2000: 14). The first is an improvisation with the whole company, based on an *auto-cours* from the school, where the entire group of thirty students combine to imagine and act out a 24-hour cycle of a place, like a town square or village (Lecoq, 2000: 96–7). We will then introduce perhaps Lecoq's most well-known exercise, 'The Seven Levels of Tension', and offer up some examples of how it can be deployed towards defining and refining the world of the play. To end this chapter, we will sink our teeth into the more abstract or 'essentialized' work from the study of the 'universal poetic awareness' (Lecoq, 2000: 45), with light, colours and paintings.

A day in the life of the play

When rehearsing a Shakespeare play the director will usually want the company to get a sense of the world of the play. This is often done through research – different members of the company being assigned a different aspect of life in the period in which the production is set, or sometimes the world of the play is presented to the company by the director and designer and the actors find a way to fit into it. This exercise, however, is designed to provide a physical, visceral, ensemble experience of the world of the play. It is based on an *auto-cours* where the whole class, at the Lecoq school, joins forces to recreate the day in the life of a particular place:

> Their task is to represent the life of a square in a village or small market town in France from dawn to nightfall. The students have to feel, and make us feel, the rhythmic progression of life in the course of one complete day, carrying out all the actions which could really take place: cleaning, encounters in the street, shopping, meals, the Mass, the market etc. (Lecoq, 2000: 96)

Julius Caesar

- Imagine you are working on *Julius Caesar*. A key scene at the beginning of the play takes place on a festival day called Lupercalia.

- Your task is, as an ensemble, to recreate as realistically as you can Rome on the day of the Lupercalia.

- You will need to do some basic research into the nature of the Lupercalia. Much of what happened on the Feast of Lupercal can only be imagined, but starting from some research from a reliable source, you can build up an idea of how the various types of people and animals may have behaved throughout the course of the day.

- Allot roles within the company. There should be as wide a representation as you can muster, from slaves to priests, young and old, men and women, and animals.

- Allow the actors a certain amount of time to figure out what the person they are representing might do throughout the whole day. Different people (and animals, should you wish to play them too) will feature at different times in the day.

- Individual actors may want to team up with others and can recruit objects or furniture from the rehearsal space to help them bring to life their journey in any way they like. If you prepare this over a number of days, invite actors to bring in whatever costume or props they can muster to help them replay the day.

- At a given time, clear the space and let the actors improvise their way through a version of a day in Rome on the Feast of Lupercal. It will be chaotic, no doubt, and very confusing for everyone involved. It will need someone with a sharp eye to watch it all and make some sense of what is happening.

- When the day has been acted out, gather to discuss what has been achieved and then adapt what you have done to play through it again, and over the next few days, you can refine what is happening until you have a version of the day you are happy with.

- The beauty of this exercise (and it took two weeks for Lecoq's students to work on it) is that it is all about creating detail that will underpin the world you are creating for the play itself; an embodied, collective, dynamic back-story for the play, details of which might or might not make their way into the production.

- For the same play, *Julius Caesar*, you could create the day in the life of the Roman forum or even the day in the life of Brutus' army camp to serve similar purposes.

Adapt this exercise to the play you are working on. If it is *Hamlet,* then what is the everyday routine of the castle of Elsinore? If you are working with *Henry IV, Part 1 or Part 2,* then you may want to examine the day in the life of the tavern in Eastcheap, where Falstaff and his cronies drink and it would be fascinating to live through the daily routine of Duke Senior's court in his Forest of Arden exile from *As You Like It.*

The Seven Levels of Tension

'The Seven Levels of Tension' is a way of using your body to change how you act, think, feel and play by changing muscle tension. Lecoq discusses his development of the method in the *Theatre of Movement and Gesture* (2006: 89) where he speaks of the levels as each suiting 'a different style of theatre' (2006: 89). 'The Seven Levels of Tension' is most frequently used as an exercise for working on character. You can, however, take any aspect of a Shakespeare production and try it in different levels of tension to increase your options. Getting familiar with levels of tension gives you an immediate and embodied alternative to thinking and talking, which, is a very good thing to have as a shorthand in an ensemble, as new things can be tried without getting 'bogged down,' in 'a huge amount of discussion' (Lloyd, 2022). 'Seven Levels of Tension' is also a highly effective tool in exploring the world of the play with the whole company. Phyllida Lloyd made extensive use of tension levels in her trilogy of all-female, prison-based, Donmar Warehouse productions of *Julius Caesar, Henry IV* and *The Tempest*:

> What I did use the seven levels of tension for was an organizing principle in relation to the ensemble. So that in these particular plays, looking at individuals in relation to the group: the individual in parliament, the king in relation to the army, the person who has just landed on a desert island in relation to the islanders who have been there for an eternity. It was about creating a vocabulary in the room that everybody could

understand. And it was a short-cut avoiding psychology and high-intellectual speak or getting bogged down in a huge amount of discussion. (Lloyd, 2022)

We will lead you through a version of the Lecoq exercise and then apply it to exploring the world of the play. You will need about forty minutes to do the initial exercise which takes you from level one to level seven.

Exploring the Seven Levels of Tension

The first level of tension (which Lecoq calls sub-relaxation) (2006: 90)

- Imagine you have little or no muscular tension in your body and allow yourself to collapse on to the floor, safely. Try it several times until it becomes almost a pleasure.
- Now find some way to move across the floor in a 'collapsed' way. Roll very gently. Imagine you are like sea-weed, being wafted at the bottom of the sea.
- As you move, imagine that your eyesight, your hearing and thinking are all in a state of collapse.
- Try to make some sound in this state. You will manage no more than grunts and groans.
- Even though you are in a state of collapse, you are going to stand up. It will take about thirty seconds to a minute to come to standing. Find a way to do it with as little muscular effort as possible. Get your bottom into the air and the rest will follow. Allow yourself to be heavy. When you have stood up, fall down again, safely. Then get back up in just fifteen seconds this time.
- Move through the space as if you were just about to fall again – on the verge of collapsing.

The first level of tension is like reverting to some primal state. It takes you to a place which is out of the ordinary and opens a door into the unknown. Once you enter level one of tension, you release yourself from the normal rules of life and prepare yourself to take on new lives, unfamiliar movements, strange sounds and new connections.

- You may feel zombie-like, as if you were sleepwalking. Use this very low level of tension to feel intoxicated, as if you are barely human. It can be troubling to some and very freeing for others.
- Find a way to split the group in two and let one group continue to move around in level one of tension while the others watch.
- See what kind of space is created. It is an epic space – the space of outrageous dramatic possibility.

The second level of tension (which Lecoq calls relaxation) (2006: 90)

- Walk through the space, casually. Let your arms hang and feel an overall looseness in your walk. Allow your gaze to wander.
- Say 'hi' or 'how you doin'?' as you pass people. Just amble, with no direction. Imagine that it's a nice day; the sun is shining and all is well with the world.
- There are many ways to describe this: laid-back, unbothered. It brings a kind of confidence. Carry on moving around the space with nonchalance.
- Move a chair – lazily. Try and have a conversation with another person – it won't get far. Move on and find someone else to chat to.
- Imagine getting your phone out and scrolling; that is a good example of a level two activity – mooching.

This level may also feel ordinary. If level one is a portal from the normal world into the world of the unknown, then level two is reminder of the very normal world. It is casual.

- Have one portion of the company carry on in the space like this and let the other portion watch. See what kind of space opens up. There is a degree of chaos and a lack of energy or clear direction.

The third level of tension (which Lecoq called 'the economic body') (2006: 90)

- Move through the space with purpose. Spot somewhere on the far side of the room. Walk towards it with no other intention except to get there. Do this several times, from one side of the room to another. Be particular about this, by waiting at one wall until you have identified some object or area just above your eyeline on a far wall, and then walk directly towards it. You may have to pause or change direction momentarily to allow for someone else's journey; be calm but firm with this.

- Imagine that you want to get from one place to another without giving anything away about yourself. You are neither in a hurry nor dawdling.

- When you meet others you will greet them with a degree of formality, speak simply and move on.

- Be as simple as you can. Move a chair or table and see how simply you can do it under the influence of this third level of tension. Aim to be as efficient in your movement as possible.

- Place some chairs or stools around the room. Sit down and get up again. Move from one to another. Feel that you are more poised than normal.

- Move your arms, as you walk, a bit more than you feel is necessary. It should feel like you are holding your arms somewhat. To achieve this kind of efficiency and poise, you may feel a bit robotic; slightly military even.

This is the state of neutrality, and unlike a car in neutral, which will go nowhere, this neutral is active, and not only is it active, but it is also not natural. It is the state of finding the right energy for the job: no less, no more.

- Arrange it so that one-half of the company moves through the space in level three of tension and the others watch. There will be straight lines and a sense of order. There will be a faint feeling of mystery about it as if drama could happen, but it is not happening yet.

The fourth level of tension (which Lecoq called 'the supported body') (2006: 90)

- Move through the space with a spring in your step.
- Look out of the windows, into the corners of the space and at the other people with interest. Be fascinated by what is around you. Be curious about everything.
- Skip around the space for a while and then walk normally but feel that you are still skipping somehow. Do some of the activities that you did with chairs in level three with this liveliness.
- Point at things and name them like a child might do. Become absorbed by something that delights you, on your own or with someone else.
- Allow sounds to come out of you. It may be an 'oh' or an 'ah' at something you see. It could be a 'wow' at what someone else is doing. Whistle a tune. Whistling, like skipping is a wonderful conduit for this playful state.

The fourth level of tension is one of play. It is crucial to all our theatrical endeavours. Lecoq described it as 'the level of the realistic theatre' (2006: 90). He also called it the level of clowning. For Lecoq a degree of lightness, playfulness and pleasure was crucial to acting. It is the essential state of make-believe. Without it, there is no imagining that you are anything other than yourself.

- Divide the group so one-half watches the other half moving through the space in level four. What kind of space opens up? A varied, busy, unpredictable space. A space where anything can happen.

The fifth level of tension (which Lecoq called 'the first muscular tension') (2006: 90)

- Move through the space and imagine that the air is thicker than it is. Imagine that here is resistance to your moving, in all directions.
- Crouch down but imagine there is a cushion of air beneath you.

- Reach up above and feel that the air is pushing back.
- Try and spin around but feel that you will have to take a bit more time to do it because the thick air is holding you back.
- Include your legs in this exploration. Play a game where you must drag your feet a bit when you walk. Try to kick the air, but imagine your leg is impeded by thick foam.
- Stand for a moment and then feel that, as you are moving forwards, you are also unsticking your back from an imagined sticky wall. Do the same in other directions, going sideways, down and up. Treat it as a purely physical game for the moment.

Even when treated simply as a physical game, you will probably start to feel different – emotionally and psychologically – as you do these movements. If not, try again and see if you can let the movement suggest an inner state. The physical change, which is a general tightening of the muscles, leads to an emotional and psychological shift in the actor. The more you practice these psycho-physical strategies the more the mind and the body will play as one.

Level five is the level of suspense.

- Imagine that you are walking on a tightrope. You progress across it one foot at a time, using your arms and free leg to find balance.

With the tension levels five and six, particularly, it is useful to feel how the sensations created by them can be broadly positive or negative. On the tightrope you may well feel positive and negative: positive in that you are defying gravity and negative in that you are afraid of falling. They are both strong feelings of suspension. Try both.

- Find someone to talk to. Improvise a conversation entirely in the fifth level of tension – in suspense. Both be positive. Both be negative and then swap the positive and negative between you.
- Divide the group so one-half watches the other half moving through the space in level five. What kind of space opens up? A held, tense, space, fraught with possibilities, both good and bad.

The sixth level of tension (which Lecoq called 'the second muscular tension') (2006: 90)

Level six of tension is physically demanding. Only do it in short bursts until you have found a way to sustain it.

- Move through the space energetically. This will involve jumping, kicking, rushing, spinning and moving fast.
- Burst your way out of an imagined container. Keep bursting. Burst open all over the place. Make it fun. It is a game, but move with urgency. It is almost chaotic and bordering on being violent.
- Try having a full-on punch-up with yourself. It's impossible. It's a game but it will give you a taste of the high stakes of level six of tension.
- Now explode like a series of fireworks, complete with sounds. Move your whole body. Level six of tension is like a series of explosions that are contained like steam in a steam engine.

Here is a level six game from the great clown and actor Marcello Magni:

- Imagine that you are all waiting for 'the most important person in the universe' to arrive. At a given signal, you all burst into level six of tension at the same time, using the whole body and full voice, to instruct, point, urge, move furniture and re-arrange the space for 'the most important person in the universe' with maximum volatility.
- Remember that it is a game. It does not need to be realistic or make sense. It is designed to get you to feel very high stakes, collectively, through your bodies.
- Play out the same scenario, as abovementioned example, but this time fill it with joy, laughter and exuberance.

The key to this sixth level of tension is to imagine that there is a force from beyond you that you can only just control, making you move somewhat wildly. Your job is to release it and then contain it; it should feel like you are riding a wild horse. Level six is passionate action, as in a fight or a sex scene; it is fiery.

The seventh level of tension (which Lecoq called 'the third muscular tension') (2006: 90)

The seventh level of tension is where action loses its power. It is the place where the situation, either internal for the character or external in terms of events, or most likely, a combination of the two, has become so overwhelming that human behaviour can no longer hold sway.

- Choose a simple movement: turning around, stretching out an arm, bending a leg. While staying in place, take the movement as far as it will go until you find yourself in some sort of extreme shape. Hopefully you will come to a position where it will feel that you are, for example, completely twisted, utterly stretched out or hopelessly compromised. You will be in a position from which you feel that no more action can take place. You have, in effect, exhausted yourself but you have a shape in space that contains and conveys the exhaustion.

- Do it again but with a new movement so that you reach a new shape.

- Split the room so you can watch one-half of the company do it at a time. See what kind of space opens up. It may be epic again, like the first level of tension. It's as if we have almost come full circle.

- You will see shapes of desperation, ultimatum, tragedy, humiliation, reaching, reaching for an answer which maybe only the gods have. It is the point of no return.

Although Lecoq describes the levels of tension in *Theatre of Movement and Gesture* (as cited earlier), he does so so enigmatically, as to not be that practically useful. The names that Lecoq gives to the levels there are vague and do not give a clear sense of the emotional or physical state, so we offer up a few generic words for them, many based on his teaching. However, it is wise to get used to using the numbers to ensure that your interpretation of each level of tension is as wide and open as possible.

1. Hypotension. Collapsing. Desperate.
2. Relaxed. Nice. Easy.

3.   Neutral. Purposeful. Active. Economical.
4.   Playful. Curious. Song-like.
5.   In suspense. Tense. On edge.
6.   Passionate. Full-on. Explosive.
7.   Hypertension. Epic. Frozen.

Connecting to Shakespeare (levels of tension)

One of the many reasons that theatre-makers come back to Shakespeare's plays over and over is that they offer up so many worlds to explore. But, of course, once the specific world that Shakespeare wrote about is negotiated, then there is an almost limitless way of connecting to that world from our contemporary vantage point.

Using 'The Seven Levels of Tension' to think creatively about framing the world of the play

- Think about the space of the play.

This is more than physical locations. For instance, in *Hamlet*, a couple of 'spaces' could be (a) a political infrastructure under attack and (b) a psychological world of grief.

- Then start to contemplate the spaces in relation to the levels of tension. Be methodical about this. Take one level of tension at a time and imagine the spaces of play through the prism of the tension level. Try all the levels, even if you do not think, to start with, that some of them will be suitable or useful. Using the levels of tension to frame your thinking will open up fresh and creative possibilities for the world of your play.

Here is an example how you might go about this in relation to *The Comedy of Errors,* using just a selection of tension levels, even though we recommend that you try all levels in relation to the play you are working on. We will take it that key examples of physical and thematic spaces in the play are (a) a market town and (b) mistaken identity.

Tension level: Three

Words, ideas and sensations connected to level three include: straightforward, efficient and neutral.

Associated creative thinking: Once you start exploring the space of the play with level three, it may well lead to aspects of realism. The things that people (merchants, goldsmiths and servants, for example) do in the market town become paramount. Details of materials will present themselves and the actuality of how things are sold and made will engage the company. In level three, mistaken identity is stripped somewhat of its emotions, as level three is neutral. This helps in plotting the mechanics of the confusions. The more clearly the company understands the details of the mistaken identities, the more comedy can come from the audience's appreciation of the predicament, rather than from pushing the superficial energy of it.

Reflections on world of play: A place of work and realistic details where the logic of the mistaken identities underpins the farcical elements.

Tension level: Six

Words, ideas and sensations connected to level six include: passionate action, full-on and explosive.

Associated creative thinking: Level six brings with it a high-energy and so it might suggest a very physicalized comedy universe. It suggests the possibility of the audience being almost assaulted by the play, like Dromio of Ephesus is assaulted by Antipholus of Syracuse. The market, mixed with explosive energy, might promote a world in which the audience is being invited into the maelstrom of a middle-eastern bazaar, leading to possibilities of an immersive staging. Level six exists in a world of chaos and so the mistaken identities that drive the comedy are borne out of a viscerally chaotic energy.

Reflections on world of play: chaotic, cacophonous and highly physical.

Tension level: One

Words, ideas and sensations connected to level one include: collapsing, desperate and blurred.

Associated creative thinking: Level one is extreme. As soon as you start framing your thinking about Ephesus from the perspective of level one of tension, or almost no tension at all, the place will start to appear dream-like and unreal. The sounds, smells and heat of the place will take over. The sense of overwhelm that comes from this will help to drive the play. In terms of mistaken identity, level one will bring out the sense of derangement attached to it. Level one affords a kind of melt-down. In level one, the body almost melts away and so it will push your choices around the mistaken identities to a point where the humans involved feel like they are almost disintegrating.

Reflections on world of play: Level one brings out a kind of dream-like or nightmarish quality, and could possibly ratchet up the aural and olfactory qualities of the setting as well as the visual. It could lead to music, and visuals being distorted and unsettling.

The levels of tension are not only great for exploring the playing of the story but also very useful in framing your initial thinking about the world of the play too. Level two could bring out a kind of chumminess in the play's relationships, level four could highlight the almost fantastical nature of the play, level five the fear of not knowing what is going on, and seven the pain of dislocation. As ever, we encourage an ensemble approach. To really embrace the Lecoq ethos, do the these contemplations in an ensemble environment, in a space where you can move easily, and where there is access to a variety of objects, costumes and musical instruments.

Improvising with levels of tension in
A Midsummer Night's Dream

To give you a clearer idea of how to explore the levels of tension in relation to one aspect of the world of the play, we will lay out an example of the sort of thing you could be doing with tension-level improvisation. We have chosen the world of the 'rude mechanicals' from *A Midsummer Night's Dream,* to give you an idea of how this works before you activate this strong tool on your own production or scene study. For guidance on this kind of group improvisation, go to Chapter 2 and see section 'Connecting to Shakespeare (improvisation)'.

Read the following and insert a world from your play.

- Gather the personnel who will be most suited to exploring the world of the 'rude mechanicals' and, of course this may well contain the actors who will be playing these parts in the production.

- Choose a scene in which the mechanicals appear. For the sake of ease, we will choose, for this example, the scene in which they rehearse the play (3.1), in part, because it was the scene that inspired Lecoq to set the *auto-cours* of 'Clowns Rehearsing a Play' at the school.

- Do a warm-up of the seven levels to re-familiarize.

- Ask each of the actors to reflect briefly on what their character is doing in the scene.

- Depending on personnel and skill levels, take as much time as it feels appropriate, to explore the scene, in your own words, allowing space for moments, play and diversions that are not in the play to appear.

- The actors will now improvise the scene, in all seven levels of tension, in order to delve into the world of the 'rude mechanicals'. We have laid out some possible outcomes in the following examples with just four tension levels but please consider using all seven yourselves.

In this exercise, all the performers will be in the same level of tension for each improvisation. This is the challenge. It will often appear to not make any sense in terms of the play you are doing, or for certain characters, who you imagine would never be in that tension level. You will feel the natural desire to shift into other registers or levels; resist this for the time being. Also note that levels one and two are more for exploration than rehearsal or performance. Level seven is very demanding to maintain for performance, and only the most highly stylized theatre could be said to employ it. This kind of improvisation should be done early in the process if you are using it to define the world of the play itself. Here is a selection of examples of what might occur.

Tension level: Three

- Qualities of the tension level include: order, clarity and action.
- Possible playing outcomes: The rude mechanicals will appear more serious. It will create an interesting shift of balance in the whole play, as these characters, often seen as foolish, will gain a degree of dignity and straightforwardness. Level three will bring out what they are good at, so it may be that their respective trades, as weavers, carpenters and so on will be accentuated.
- Notes on reflections on the world created: The world of work. Dignity. Even more comedy as they take themselves more seriously.

Tension level: Five

- Qualities of the tension level include: anticipation, worry and hope.
- Possible playing outcomes: Like level three, this level is not an easy match with the 'rude mechanicals' which makes it all the more enticing to attempt. This could go in two key directions. First, the suspense of not knowing how to do what they have to do could lead to a kind of painful hesitation, or the suspense of wanting so much to be performing for the court could lead to a precipitousness in all of their actions.
- Notes on reflections on the world created: Improvising with this tension level might lead to reflecting on the social class or economic status of these characters, in relation, particularly, to court. Therefore, the reality of their position in society might become a key to their world.

Tension level: One

- Qualities of the tension level include: collapse and disintegration.
- Possible playing outcomes: Putting the mechanicals into a world where they are disintegrating, collapsing and barely

conscious might throw up all sorts of possibilities. Lecoq suggest a couple of images for this level in *Theatre of Movement and Gesture*. One is 'sea-birds tarred up on the beach' (2006: 90). It is a truly pathetic image. It could be interesting to explore the pathetic and hopeless in relation to this funny world of clowns. Lecoq also says it is the level of 'muttering and swearing to oneself', revealing, perhaps, a dark undertow to these seemingly silly characters (2006: 90).

- Notes on reflections on the world created: Desperation. Poverty.

Tension level: Two

- Qualities of the tension level include: relaxation.
- Possible playing outcomes: This world is a more relaxed world in general than that of the court with which it contrasts. The relaxation and bonhomie of this level might suggest a kind of closeness with the audience. The mechanicals might emerge from among the audience in this level of tension. Improvising this world in level two is likely to bring out the friendliness of these people towards one another. It will highlight the possibility of their generosity and easiness.

- Notes on reflections on the world created: A world at one with the space or theatre you are presenting it in. Level two could suggest an almost casual, friendly, relationship between mechanicals and audience.

After you have done these improvisations, you will be in a much stronger position to make decisions about space, set, music and style of playing. This work could, of course, be done at a research and development stage, weeks or months before you start rehearsing.

It is also useful to use the levels of tension, in this way, when you have made decisions about the world and how to stage the play.

Exploring the texture of the play via colours and paintings

In further exploration of the world of the play, we turn to one of Lecoq's most iconic strategies, which forms a part of the journey into what Lecoq called the 'universal poetic awareness' (2000: 47): the movement of colour. The movement of colour is about as abstract a strategy as the pedagogy offers, but, at the same time, is it also accessible, and once felt, powerful and useful. Lecoq explains the 'universal poetic awareness' in *The Moving Body:*

> Here we are dealing with an abstract dimension, made up of spaces, lights, colours, materials, sounds which can be found in all of us. They have been laid down in all of us by our various experiences and sensations, by everything we have seen, heard, touched, tasted. All the things are there inside us, and constitute the common heritage, out of which will spring dynamic vigour and the desire to create. Thus my teaching method has to lead to this universal poetic awareness in order not to limit itself to life as it is. (2000: 47)

A theatre production, Shakespeare or otherwise, will often have a distinctive palate of colour in its design, but what we are suggesting with colour, in this section, is, inevitably, concerned with movement. Lecoq states in *The Moving Body* that 'there is a tempo, a space, a rhythm which is exactly right for each colour' (2000: 49). In a Lecoq-influenced ensemble approach, colour may well be treated as something that inspires the collective in terms of music, design and performance. As ever, the way of understanding colour is to embody it. In this section we will guide you through processes to embody lights and colours, with an example of how embodying paintings or the style of a particular painter can inform your choice of world.

Playing with colour

Of embodying colours, Lecoq is economical when he explains his process in *The Moving Body:*

> With the students in small groups, I call out different colours and ask them to react as rapidly as possible, without thinking, expressing the internal movement they feel. I run through all the colours of the rainbow, they then choose colours they can see in the studio and suggest movements for them. The onlookers

then try and identify the colours which have been presented. (2000: 48)

We will need to be a bit more explicative to help you into your journey of embodying colours.

Yellow

- Spread out in your space. Think of the colour **yellow**.
- Notice how it makes you feel. What associations do you have with it. Notice how that makes you want to move. Yellow often creates feelings of lightness and openness.
- Imagine that you have a magic paintbrush and imagine what it would be like to 'paint' the space yellow. This will involve large, whole-body movements. They might feel almost like a dance, with a strong flavour of whatever yellow feels like to you.
- Find a partner and take a few moments to share notes about what you felt and what you did.

Blue

- Stop in a new place and come to a neutral standing position and think of the colour **blue**. You will be highly likely to have a different response to this colour than yellow.
- Start to move through the space as if you are the colour blue.

The word 'blue' has many cultural associations. 'The blues' is a particular kind of soulful music borne out of hardship. The Virgin Mary was often depicted in blue in Renaissance paintings as lapis lazuli was the most expensive dye. It is also the colour of a cloudless sky. Lecoq was at pains to attempt to invite his students, who came from very diverse cultural and geographical backgrounds, to move as *the colour itself* as opposed to the cultural associations of the colour:

I am particularly attentive to the quality of their [students] movements. I can tell whether the movements arise from their own bodies or from an external image, a sort of picture postcard which they are trying to illustrate, or again if they are doing a symbolic movement, giving us an external representation of the colour they are trying to describe to us. (Lecoq, 2000: 49)

You may not come to as clear a definition as Lecoq came to about colours and how they move, but if your group all move in relation to blue you are highly likely to have a consensus on roughly how it moves. If nothing else, make sure that it is different from the movement of yellow.

- Spend a few moments, up to a minute or two, exploring how blue manifests in movement for you and then find another person to move with. Improvise with them. You can go with what they do, or contrast what they do. You might feel that you are leading or following what your partner does.

Red

- Go through the same stages as the previous example but with the colour **red.**
- Move freely through the space as if 'painting' the space red.

Lecoq is very specific about red. He explains: 'the students who choose red often make explosive movements. Now as soon as the explosion is over the colour drains out of the movement and turns into pure light. True red only exists just before the explosion, the powerful dynamic tension of the instant' (2000: 49). Red needs to be maintained like level six of tension – almost like a continuous set of mini explosions.

- Keep comparing notes with others. Despite the seemingly prescriptive tone Lecoq takes, it is vital to consider your own experience of the colours.
- You can, of course, go on to explore the whole range of colours. You can mix the movement of red and yellow and enter into a whole new world of orange! The mix of blue and yellow of course, leads to green, which is distinct from both its parent colours.
- You can then explore shades of colours (light blue is very different from dark blue), according to your tastes and needs.

- You should also attempt to embody white and black in movement. These, you might argue, are more variations of light than colour per se, and very useful as such.

Lecoq actually precedes the work on colour with light, and so without going into too much detail, before you attempt the painting exercise which follows, you could usefully explore how different kinds of light move.

Moving like light

At the beginning of the journey into what Lecoq calls the 'universal poetic awareness' (2000: 47) students will be invited to move in ways that suggest different kinds of light.

- Walk through the space. Now imagine that you have a large lamp, like a car headlight on your chest. Carry on moving through the space with this in mind. The imagined light clears a path ahead of you. You might also imagine that the beam of light travels all the way through you so that you are suspended by and on a strong, fat beam of light.

- Imagine then that you have beam of light coming from your face. It will have a similar effect as the chest light but now you can manoeuvre it with some agility with your neck. You may well have the impression of spaces opening up around you.

- Now imagine that you have lights on the palms of your hands and explore your ability to shine light from your hands into ever more various places.

- Contrast this with a lack of light. See what happens to you when you imagine not letting any light out. You may stand inert. You may curl up somewhat. An impression of deepest darkness might make you reduce intensely like some kind of human negative space.

- Embody the following light types to the best of your ability. You may be surprised once you start how much easier it is than you first imagine. Make movements with your whole body. Allow it to take more time than you think it should.

1. The dappled light of the sun shining through the leaves of a tree.
2. The flickering on of a neon light.
3. Morning light slanting through the slats in a venetian blind.
4. The light of an outdoor heater.
5. The swirling light of a police siren.
6. The dull light of an overcast day.
7. The light of stars in the night sky.
8. The light of a candle in a dark room.

Be playful with the abovementioned. You may well find yourself making gestures which suggest something of the shape of the object that makes or affects the quality of light. For instance, in 'dappled light' the leaves and trunk of trees may appear in your mind's eye in some way. The long straight tube of the *neon light* will affect how you move, as will the slats of the *venetian blind* making you stop and start slightly as the light is clearly punctuated and differentiated by imagining the slats through which the light appears. Make your first effort to be to capture and portray, to the best of your ability, the particular type of light we have suggested. We have filmed an example of this in Video 4: https://bloomsbury.pub/shakespeare-and-lecoq

Exploring paintings

Using paintings is a common way for designers to garner inspiration for a Shakespeare production. Peter Brook made a memorable debut at the Stratford Memorial Theatre, in 1946, with a wistful production of *Love's Labour's Lost,* inspired by the paintings of Watteau while the 1981 BBC Shakespeare production of *All's Well That Ends Well,* directed by Elijah Moshinsky, used Rembrandt's influence to great effect. Grace Godwin notes that in 2016, no less than three of the RSC's productions – *Hamlet* (dir. Simon Godwin), *Doctor Faustus* (dir. Maria Aberg) and *The Alchemist* (dir. Polly Findlay) were inspired by the post-modern artist Jean-Michel Basquiat (2017).

Lecoq's specific use of paintings takes us into the abstract once again, but an abstraction whose purpose is to guide the ensemble to new insights which come from play, space and movement rather than from cogitation. Lecoq explains himself how he has to wrangle his own students away from their habitual thinking patterns to find new ways of applying themselves creatively:

> The pedagogical task is to isolate digressive movement without ever indicating what should be done instead. I have to create a state of uncertainty; it's up to the student to discover what the teacher already knows. The teacher must be prepared, at every moment, to question his own approach, to get back to the world with freshness, and innocence to avoid imposing clichés. (2000: 49)

The paintings *auto-cours* task at the Lecoq school is to recreate a painting in movement: 'From analysing colours, students go on to work in a more integrated way on a whole painting. . . . It is not a matter of illustrating the picture, nor of explaining how they see it but of sharing in a direct way, the spirit of the work' (Lecoq, 2000: 49).

Recreating a painting in movement

- As previously in the book, assemble a group of actors, play games and warm yourselves up especially with light and colours before you attempt this task.

- You will need a visual aid of a painting. This can be done in a number of ways, but it is vital to have a version of a painting in front of you (and once you have got the hang of the exercise, it could easily be a sculpture or photograph too).

- Take a few minutes to look at the painting but do not over-discuss it. Find a large space to move about in and set about improvising with the colours, light, lines, shapes of the painting. This will involve people diving in and making suggestions in movement.

- Somebody may well take the lead and others will follow. Individuals may take responsibility for a colour each. There is no absolute prescription for this process, and Lecoq would certainly never have imposed one.

- The colours, light, lines and shapes will dictate what you do to an extent, and the painting's subject matter will almost inevitably creep into your movement work too but as Lecoq counsels earlier, 'It is not a matter of illustrating the picture, nor of explaining how they see it but of sharing in a direct way, the spirit of the work' (2000: 47).

- At first, the painting can be brought to life in a pure way, without it needing to be connected to the play.

- The world of the play will be in the back of the performers' minds and the minds of those who are watching. Any ideas of how the world of this painter will impact and inspire the world of the play (alongside, of course, Shakespeare's words, situations and setting) will occur almost as a by-product of doing the exercise.

- Set a time limit for the group to make a movement piece and if you have warmed up you will be able to make an attempt on this in about twenty to forty minutes, depending on your experience. A good amount of people for one painting is around five to seven.

- As you do this, you can discuss things as you go, but keep discussion to a minimum so that you keep to the task of embodying rather than intellectualizing.

- Keep improvising and then stop to discuss what seems to work and then go back to more and more structured improvising as the minutes pass. You do not need to come up with a finished piece but see if you can find something which feels to you as if it has some sort of beginning, middle and end, or a sense of journey about it.

- This kind of movement work is fundamentally abstract, even if you choose a figurative painting. The group movement which you will make only has to convey the spirit of the painting and not the realistic detail, so there is no need to act anything out but instead to move in what will feel, to actors, more like dance than drama.

- A movement piece based on a painting might last up to a minute or even longer, which, in turn, is longer than you will normally take to look at a painting. This is a '*transposition*' (see Chapter 1 p. 21). You are recreating something in a different medium, a fundamentally creative process.

- After twenty minutes or half an hour, show the piece, or pieces, to the rest of the company. This will excite discussion about the connection of the painting and the artist to the world of the play you are putting on.

- It depends, of course, on your project, what you do next. If the artist or painting was a good choice and chimes with the company in terms of how you feel the world of the play can emerge, you will be led by it, towards considerations of:

  a. playing spaces
  b. relationship to the audience
  c. rhythm
  d. costume
  e. set
  f. music

All of this, now, has the potential to be in the domain of the company rather than just with the director. The company is empowered by a connection to elements of the 'poetic matrix' of the show, and the director, designer and composer have an embodied, moving, spatial or 'plastic', as Lecoq would often say, artefact (the movement piece) to propel their ideas from.

Connecting further to Shakespeare (using paintings for differentiating worlds within the play)

Many of Shakespeare's plays have contrasting worlds within them. *Romeo and Juliet* opposes the Montagues and Capulets for its drama, *Troilus and Cressida* pitches the revengeful Greeks, against the besieged Trojans, and of course, *A Midsummer Night's Dream* has arguably three separate worlds: that of Theseus' court and the young lovers, that of the 'rude mechanicals' trying to put on a play and that of the fairies.

The two worlds The Winter's Tale

- Think of your play and choose two distinct locales or world within it. *The Winter's Tale* has two very obviously contrasting worlds, that of Leontes' court (Sicilia) and the home of the Shepherds (Bohemia).

- Choose two different paintings ideally from two different artists which seem to encapsulate something essential to the way you understand each of the worlds.

- Split the company in two and give each of the groups a painting each to explore in the way we have described earlier.

- For our example we have chosen two relatively well-known paintings to help get the idea across, one by Egon Schiele *Self-portrait with Chinese Lantern and Fruits* (1912) and the other by Jean-Honoré Fragonard; *The_Swing* (1767).

The first is a graphically exposing nude, with a dirty-white background. The flesh tones are charcoally and there is a dot of vivid red for his lip. It is sparse, with the lines of the body being done very sparingly. There is a coil of lines, resembling barbed wire on one arm, and the hair on the head and pubis are dark splodges. The second is a large, lushly colourful, prettily detailed masterpiece of the rococo period celebrating a romanticized moment of a young woman on the swing being marvelled at by a young man crouching in the corner of the canvas. She is depicted in blazing light, with ruffles of lace and pink. The movement pieces for the two paintings will be very different and in this case the harsh lines and stark background of the Schiele will create movements which will connect immediately with the paranoid and touchy mental space that Leontes creates, while the lushness and detail of the Fragonard will open up all sorts of possibilities to do with the humour, freedom and fun of the shepherds' world.

- Once each group makes a movement piece based on the paintings, discuss each in terms of all creative pathways that we have mentioned earlier.

There are two key ways to get more out of the process. One is to reverse the inspiration. This means to apply the work to a painting which seems, on the surface, not to chime with the world of the play. In our example, this would be to use the Schiele painting for the shepherds and the Fragonard for the court . This will bring out a kind of counter-reality in the worlds. The other is to randomize your choice so that you pick a painting almost by chance and apply it to the world of the play to see what emerges. For instance, you might take Hockney's famous Californian swimming pool painting (*A Bigger Splash*, 1967) into the process of rehearsing *A Winter's Tale* and see how you can collectively surprise yourselves about to how the calm, slightly surreal sense of mystery in that painting could inspire the company into creating some interesting choices for this play.

5

Exploring the text

One of the difficulties of acting Shakespeare, or any text, is that it has been written down. As soon as it is written down, it becomes part of something that is connected to literature, which can lead to an intellectual approach to the text more suited to the classroom than in the rehearsal studio. We are, therefore, going to recruit some of Lecoq's pedagogy, in this chapter, to help you to find the pleasure in individual words, the need to speak them and the gestural life that underpins them.

When Phyllida Lloyd was building her ensemble for her all-female Donmar Trilogy, she reflected on the fact that she was 'thinking really seriously about movement in the rehearsal room because, in this country [Britain] there has been a tendency to perform Shakespeare from the neck up' (Lloyd, 2022). This might seem like a cliché but we would argue, as does Lloyd, that the phenomenon of heady Shakespeare is to do with our 'clinging to *our* language'. It was not until Lloyd experienced ensemble Shakespeare, produced by a Russian company, that she could tell that there was an alternative to the sort of 'stiff, text-is-all, the body-limps-along-behind' way of doing Shakespeare (Lloyd, 2022). Nearly all of the companies featured in this book have been influenced by or do Shakespeare in a language other than English.

In this chapter, we will lead you through

a) a process of embodying individual words,

b) a number of possibilities for embodying Shakespeare's rhetoric and stylistic choices, and

c) embodying speeches and dialogues.

Embodying words

Words are considered, at the Lecoq school, to begin with, as part of the sequence of learning which concerns itself with what Lecoq calls 'the universal poetic awareness' (2000: 47). He elucidates: 'we consider words as living organisms; thus we search for the body of words' (2000: 50). Whether it is verbs, 'bearers of action' or nouns, 'which represent a designated object', the search, at the school, for the best learning outcomes, is for words with a 'real physical dynamic' (Lecoq, 2000: 50). Much in the same way as with colours, Lecoq's strategy is to put the words in front of the students and ask them to find movement (shape, form and rhythm) to represent the word in space.

In a similar way to that in which Shakespeare's characters speak their innermost thoughts openly, Lecoq sought to lead his students to externalize the dynamics of words. This is done, in movement, as a way of creating an embodied reality for the word, which, in turn, creates a 'trace' that will 'remain inscribed' in the actor, which is then 'reactivated in him in the moment of interpretation' (Lecoq, 2000: 46).

Exploring the physical dynamics of individual words

Verbs

Verbs or 'bearers of action' (Lecoq, 2000: 50) are the most accessible words to embody as it is usually possible to discern a bodily movement for an action. Simple verbs that Lecoq suggests being embodied, in *The Moving Body* are 'to take, to raise, to break, to saw' (2000: 50).

- Spread out through the room and nominate a member of the company to read out the following words. Without thinking, do the first thing that comes to you, on impulse.
  - Take
  - Raise
  - Break
  - Saw

- Repeat the process but take more time with it and include more of your body. As with the undulation in the first chapter, try and include as much of your body as possible, starting from the ground up.

- Say each of the words, 'Take', 'Raise' and so on with the movement you have found for it. See how the doing of the movement can simultaneously stretch or change the vocalization of word for you.

- Say the words again, but this time without the movement.

- Notice what it feels like to say the words after you have embodied them. Do they have more body? Are they more dynamic? Are the consonants crisper?

Connecting to Shakespeare: Verbs

- Take the text you are working on and pick out all the verbs and embody them by making a gesture for each of them. Here is an example to try now:

  If music **be** the food of love **play** on.

  Give me excess of it, that **surfeiting**

  The appetite may **sicken** and so **die**.

  (*TN*, 1.1.1-3)

We have picked out the verbs for you in bold.

- Try embodying the verbs with just your hand to start with. **Be** for example, might involve holding out your hand out and closing the fingers a bit; **play** could create a kind of wiggling of the fingers, **give**, an open hand, **surfeiting**, a pulsing, **sicken**, a droop, and with **die**, your hand may close up completely.

- Now try the speech, letting the sound of the words be stretched and changed by the hand gestures on each verb.

- Do the text again but this time exaggerate the hand gestures.

- Then expand this to using the whole of your body. **Be** might create a spreading of arms and legs which then a slight coming together; like a small *éclosion* from Chapter 1. **Play** might involve the whole body in a wiggle, **give** could be a leaning forward and opening the arms, etc.

- Now do the speech with the full body movements on the verbs. Allow the movements to affect the sound of the words, even if the sound of the words starts to become odd or unusual.

You are renegotiating your relationship with the words via your impulsive and intuitive sensibility. Do not be surprised if you find yourself moving in ways that are not appropriate for how you think you will perform. You can make noises at this point which are out of your normal register.

- Finally do a version of the speech without any of the physical movements and notice how the qualities of the movements have found their way into your voice.

Lecoq's exercises with words are to help you to find a 'relation' to them and not an interpretation. (Lecoq, 2000: 146). Focusing your attention on the verbs in Shakespeare's plays is a tried and tested way to accentuate the narrative pulse of the play. To embody the verbs, in preparation, will only add to the dynamic thrust of the verse.

Nouns

Words that denote objects and things are not quite so obviously mimeable. In *The Moving Body*, Lecoq gives the example of the Eiffel Tower:

Looking at the Eiffel Tower, each of us can sense a dynamic combining rootedness with an upward surge, having nothing to do with the temptation to give a picture of the monument (a figurative mime). (2000: 48)

- Try this now. Stand up and create a movement that includes a sense of 'rootedness with an upward surge'. Notice that your first instinct is to use your hands and arms; then do it again, including more of your whole body. Now you are transposing; not trying to draw an Eiffel Tower with your body, but to find an equivalent in movement.

Shakespeare chose his words very carefully, and often it is the sound, tone, rhythm and texture of a word that earns its place in a play. Lecoq makes a shrewd observation that the French word for butter is 'le beurre' which sounds like it is already 'spread' and waiting to be eaten, whereas the English 'butter' sounds and feels more like it is still in its packet (2000: 51).

- Try making movements for these two words which represent the same thing but from different cultures.
- *Beurre* . . . has a kind of horizontal ooze to it . . .
- Butter is a bit more vertical, with squared off edges.

It is worth creating movement for any word you say, at some point, in your preparation, as it will help to situate the words as a physical necessity.

Connecting to Shakespeare: Nouns

- Go back to the first lines of *Twelfth Night* and pick out the nouns.

> If **music** be the **food** of **love,** play on.
> Give me **excess** of it, that surfeiting
> The **appetite** may sicken and so die.

(TN, 1.1.1-3)

- Take each noun one at a time and find a physicalization for it. Start with your hand. **Music** may be a conducting kind of hand, **food** a scooping hand and **love** an open hand.
- Re-do all five of them (adding **excess** and **appetite**) with your whole body.
- Say the words with the movement and then say each word without the movement. Can you feel a 'trace' of the movement or the body's *attitude* as you say the words now?

As in much of this book's instruction, what is key here is how you use the physical games to expand something, in this case, the nouns, into something that takes flight in the space around you, only to then be compressed and reduced, as you see fit, to offer to the audience the ghost or trace of the physical work in the eventual acting of it. As Lecoq says in *The Moving Body*, in relation to an undulation:

> Maximum expansion of undulation takes us to a point of balance in space, both in front, and behind. After this, we take the opposite course, reducing the same movement to the point where it is almost imperceptible from outside. We have reached the opposite limit, which consists simply in respiration, in apparent immobility. (2000: 79)

You will do well to take Lecoq's word on this matter of movement seriously and see if you can find ways of expanding your physical and vocal work to the maximum, so that they can be reduced to the minimum, having gained, potentially, more power and poetry.

Exploring the embodiment of rhetoric and stylistic devices

Antithesis

Antithesis is one of the most common forms of rhetoric used in Shakespeare. Antithesis is where two opposing or contrasting ideas are expressed in two adjoining clauses or sentences. Hamlet uses antithesis in the opening phrase of his most famous soliloquy:

> **To be,** or **not to be** – that is the question;

> (*Ham.* 3.1.55)

The two pairs of contrasting words are in bold. 'To be' is in stark contrast to 'not to be'.

One of Lecoq's mainstays of pedagogy is how ideas live in space. This is going to be very handy when addressing antithesis. Antithesis is built on opposition. The most obvious and available oppositions are those of up and down and from one side to the other or, to use a more bodily image, on one hand and on the other hand. Peter Hall talks of 'pointing' (Hall, 2003: 40) the antithesis to bring lucidity. By leaning onto the words of the antithesis, or lightly stressing them, you will help clarify your character's thought process. This will, in turn, help the audience to follow the sense.

Using movement to highlight antithesis

We will lead you through this very simple example and trust that you will take the implications of what we do into your own work. If we follow the spatial and bodily logic of the up and down, one hand/other hand procedure, you will see that the antithesis of 'To be, or not to be – that is the question', can be explored physically by simply looking up on 'to be' and looking down on 'to not be'.

To look up on 'to be' might imply hope, and to look down on 'not to be' might imply a kind of gloom, or even life in the former and death in the latter. You have, therefore, gently strengthened the oppositional antithesis of 'To be' and 'not to be' with this physicalization.

- In this example from *Hamlet,* once you have played with looking up and down, do the same but with your hand. Point up on one phrase and down on the other.
- Once you have done that, allow your whole body to be lifted up and crushed down as you explore these opposites, and by such means you will be writing the antithesis into your body.
- You might ultimately perform this moment with a very subtle variation of the eyes or breath, or a deeply committed physicalization of what it is to live and die, depending on your taste and the production's requirements.
- The same applies in a side-to-side movement. Very simple but useful is to look in one direction while saying, 'To be' and in the other with 'not to be'. Once this is lodged in your mind/body you can stick with it or let it go and trust that it will be read at some level by your audience.
- This side-to-side approach will be more useful when seeking out less obvious antitheses than 'To be or not to be'.

How many times you end up keeping the movement in your work depends on the kind of production you are in. Simple as it may sound, if you learn to use your body directionally in the space to highlight Shakespeare's rhetorical devices then you will help to make Shakespeare's complex writing more accessible to yourself, your playing partner and the audience.

Using movement to encourage complexity in the antithesis

With any movement exploration where the movement seems to go with or support the line of text, as in the previous examples of looking up and looking down, it is worth playing against the obvious choice too. It is a similar idea to exploring characters and situations in what seems, at first, to be the inappropriate level of tension, as we detailed in Chapter 4.

- Still with 'To be or not to be', invert the way you connect the direction of the look in relation to the line – looking down for 'to be' and looking up on 'to not be'. As soon as you apply this simplest of physical tasks, you invite fresh thinking and by just playing with direction of the look, you have created the possibility of new ways of interpreting the line too. 'To be' now is earth-bound and 'not to be' is heaven-facing, giving a different feel to the line.

Taking the embodiment of antithesis further

Let us take one more, slightly more complex example, before handing over to you, to seek out and embody antitheses on your own. It is also from *Hamlet* (1.3) where Ophelia hopes, in front of her brother, Laertes, who has just lectured her on her sexual behaviour, that he is not a hypocrite. We have bolded the key antithesis here:

OPHELIA
But, good my brother,
Do not as some ungracious pastors do
Show me the **steep and thorny way** to heaven
Whiles like a puffed and reckless libertine,
Himself the **primrose path of dalliance** treads

*(Ham.,*1.3.45-49)

At the simplest level, you can use the basic opposition of right and left to highlight the difference between 'steep and thorny way' and 'primrose path of dalliance', by looking or pointing in one direction for one and in the other direction for the other. But, with a mind for creative movement, you will notice the opportunity to embody 'steep and thorny way' with some difficult, spiky, and torturous movement and 'primrose path of dalliance' with a floating, sweet and non-committal moves.

- Try it now. With a book in hand, stand up and read the speech from 'But' to 'treads' and add some movement to the two bolded phrases.

- First, add some movement with just your hand, and then do it again but commit more of your whole body to it.

- As above, to invite some complexity here, reverse the movements so that you play the 'steep and thorny' line with the 'floating, sweet and non-committal' movement exploration, and the 'primrose path of dalliance' words accompanied by the 'difficult, spikey and tortuous' movements.

The movements should feel as though they go much further than you would normally dare to do in a naturalistic interpretation. This is not a prescription for how to act, but an invitation to explore the distance between the antithetical ideas, so that they lodge themselves into you at a cellular, body-based level, rather than as a cerebral game. Once you have explored the exaggerated movement you can tone it down to make it more subtle if you want to. As Lecoq says, having done the exploration, it will reside in you at some level, as 'the actors will retain the trace of this physical relationship to the text' (2000: 150), and it will be ready to see the light of day, in voice, breath, attitude or movement, when in rehearsal or performance it is needed.

And before we leave Ophelia and Laertes, it is worth mentioning that 'ungracious pastors' and 'reckless libertine' in the same passage are antithetical.

- Try acting out the 'ungracious pastor' and the 'reckless libertine' in movement. Make the movement as big and fanciful as you wish.

- Return to the text and include the movement you have invented for the two antithetical images of the 'pastor' and the 'libertine'.

- Reverse the above so that you put the movement of the libertine with the words 'ungracious pastor', and then the movement for the pastor with the words, 'reckless libertine'.

Once again, as with 'To be or not to be', we have not only exaggerated the physical life of the antithesis itself but also inverted our embodied discovery by putting the 'wrong' movement with each of the spoken images so that a degree of complexity has been created.

- Once you have physically explored the antithesis, do a version of it, which does not have the exploratory movement, and you will notice that the words are now freighted with some extra quality.

We would encourage you to learn to identify the antithesis in your texts as often as possible and underline them in your copy, then explore them physically.

Shakespearean asides and Lecoquian thought-bubbles

Although the term 'aside' is rarely found in the early printed texts of Shakespeare's plays, there are a number of lines that are clearly not intended to be heard by all the characters on stage but are spoken either to the audience or to a specific character. These lines are often marked as 'asides' in modern edited texts (though with varying degrees of consistency and consensus) and we will similarly use the term here. Lecoq delights in a similar technique for the physical performer which he calls '*mimages*':

These are a kind of 'close-up' on the character's internal dramatic state [. . .] the actor produces lightning gestures which express, through a different logic, the character's state at a given moment (a sort of physical aside commenting on one phase of the performance). (2000: 109)

- Choose an aside from the play you are doing to explore and follow the steps we suggest here.

We will use an aside from *Hamlet*. It is the beginning of Act 3 and is the first time that the King reveals his inner turmoil to the audience:

KING

O, 'tis too true.
[*aside*] How smart a lash that speech doth give my conscience!
The harlot's cheek beautied with plastering art
Is not more ugly to the thing that helps it
Than is my deed to my most painted word.
O heavy burden!

(*Ham.*, 3.1.48-53)

- Imagine you are the actor playing King Claudius.

- Break the aside into as many separate images as possible and work with as many as you feel you can, for example:

  a. smart a lash

  b. the harlot's cheek

  c. plastering art

  d. ugly

  e. painted word

  f. heavy burden

- Embody each of these images. We will give examples for the first two here.

  - 'Smart a lash' might come relatively easily. You could explore a kind of whipping motion. Start with your hand, then arm and then find a whipping motion with your whole body. Notice how it makes you feel. The outward motion that you make might trigger some sort of interior sensation.

  - 'The harlot's cheek' might present a more complex and elusive challenge. So, we will break it into three to investigate it further. The physicality of the image that Shakespeare has given Claudius at this point is concerned with (1) roughness; (2) a broken surface that is (3) clogged and covered up with paint. Here are some suggestions as to what to do:

    a. Close your eyes. Put your hand to your own cheek and imagine what it would be like if it was as Shakespeare has described.

    b. Then move in a more abstract way; a way that suggests that you are, or your body is, the 'harlot's cheek'.

c. Do not try and make a fixed body sculpture of it. Instead, allow yourself to move as you try to capture something of the essence of the thing.

d. First, be the **roughness** – an uneven movement.

e. Then embody **the broken surface** – an irregular, sporadic, sudden movement.

f. Third, find some movement for the **clogged paint** – a slow creeping movement.

g. Make all of the movements with as much of your body as possible, not just your arms.

h. Allow your breath to be affected and for sound to come out of you which relates in some way to the successive movements.

As we have shown before in the book, you now have series of movements and sounds which you can deploy in any way that suits the project or production you are working on. Henry Maynard, artistic director of Flabbergast Theatre, explained that in their production of *Macbeth,* he added *mimages* or physicalized images of story points in the Sergeant's speech at the beginning of the play where he describes the heroics of Macbeth in battle. Maynard describes how the company felt it was useful to include some descriptive movement at this point, so that an audience, unused to such complex language, might be helped into the story with the images. Henry also talks of using 'physical words' in their approach to Shakespeare. The whole ensemble explores particular words from speeches which then become a kind of physical language which can be threaded through the production (Maynard, 2022).

The physicalization from the aside could be used as stand-alone physical *mimage* to replace the lines if that suits your kind of production. The movement work on the aside could be incorporated by the actor playing Claudius into something that informs their approach to delivering the lines.

Embodying speeches and dialogue

In our way of working, we enter a text through the body. We never sit around and discuss, but adopt the mimodynamic method. (Lecoq, 2000: 146)

The 'mimodynamic method' is what we have described to you in respect of light and colour in Chapter 4 and in this chapter in relation to the movement of individual words and finally in respect of Claudius' aside about the 'harlot's cheek'. It is the skill of exploring phenomena via bodily movement. 'My teaching method', Lecoq continues, 'steers clear of any interpretation, concentrating on the constant respect for the internal dynamics of the text, avoiding all *a priori* readings' (2000: 146). He says that the interpreting is about the text's 'period, context, society, psychology or morality' (2000: 146), which he points out is ultimately the director's domain.

In this section we are focusing on the actor channelling the text through their body. Lecoq is very eloquent on this process:

> At a first stage, we make gestures as we speak the text, without worrying about its structure. All kinds of gestures emerge. The purpose of this basic work is to set the text free inside the body, so that the body does not become an obstacle. Once the text is learned, we strengthen the gestural dynamics, which are performed alone in silence. Gradually the structure of the text takes shape after its cloudy beginnings. (2000: 146)

Finding the gestural dynamics of dialogue

The following is an exercise which can be done with any piece of dialogue from Shakespeare. We will use an extract from *Othello* (2.3). Have a go at the exercise with our example and then move onto speeches and dialogue from your play. The scenario, here, is that Iago, Othello's ensign, is attempting to arouse sexual interest in Cassio, a lieutenant in Othello's garrison, for Othello's wife, Desdemona. Cassio is maintaining a position of propriety in face of the allure of his boss's wife:

IAGO
[. . .]
he hath not yet made wanton the night with her, and she is
    sport for Jove.
CASSIO
She's a most exquisite lady.
IAGO

And I'll warrant her full of game.
CASSIO
Indeed she's a most fresh and delicate creature.
IAGO
What an eye she has! methinks it sounds a parley to
   provocation. (*Othello,* 3.1.16-22)

- Have both actors in the space with someone reading in the lines.

- The first line is read aloud and the actor playing Iago is free to explore the line, in movement, in any way they like.

- Read the line several times until the actor is happy that they have discovered something.

In this instance, the actor playing Iago will respond to the sound of the words, feelings about Othello and Desdemona and about the act of sex. They will follow the images that arise. The body might buckle, open, twist, melt and harden up in response to all the impulses that might be flowing through Iago at this moment. It is an exploration of text and subtext.

- Read the next line and the second actor (Cassio) will respond in any way they like to what they hear.

- Continue this process until all the lines have been processed in this way.

- Try a version of the scene keeping the movement you have done in the scene. This will be highly stylized.

- Finally try a more natural version of the scene where you are free to move or not move.

This is a small example. Each actor can do this with all of their lines in ensemble time or on their own. The movement is not illustrative, literal or explicative but more abstract, expressionistic and connected to what is being said but also what might be being felt around the lines. A version of this scene is available to watch with this in Video 5: https://bloomsbury.pub/shakespeare-and-lecoq

Going further: Shared movement sequences

You may take this further still by linking the movements for this dialogue into a kind of dance.

- Once you have familiarized yourselves with these alternating movements, you can free yourselves to play with them and loosen up the sequence without the text being spoken. Your moves may well change as a result of doing them with your playing partner. You may find yourselves being in physical contact for some of it.

- It will start to feel like a dance. Repeat it several times without trying to fix it or create a set choreography.

- Share a silent, movement version of the dialogue with the ensemble. It will reveal much about the underlying reality of the scene.

- Now share a version where you do the text and the 'dance' at the same time.

- Do a third version where you both remain as still as possible and notice how the movement finds its way into your voices.

As Lecoq says, 'This kind of transfer allows us to discover that in theatre, the words themselves, like physical gestures, must achieve a certain level of *transposition*' (2000: 46). Shakespeare's language is so rich and complex that if actors move around a lot while saying it or listening to it, there is a risk of the power of the words being lost. We hope that is it clear, at this point, and in what follows, that much of what Lecoq has to offer in terms of his connection to Shakespeare might ultimately be conveyed in relative physical stillness. As Lecoq writes, in relation to the hero and chorus:

The objective is not to discover some sort of choreographic solution for the movements of the chorus, but to rather attain the point where the actor remains still, having experienced in his body the dynamics of the emotion and of the whole dramatic development. When an actor has been through these exercises, and recites this text, in their mind's eye, his audience will see him move, even when he stands still. (2000: 149).

6

Exploring character types

Exploring the four humours
via the elements

In *Shakespeare's Language*, David and Ben Crystal describe the theory of the humours, which governed the way in which the early modern period conceived of emotion, physicality and behaviour:

> In early accounts of human physiology, a person's physical and mental disposition was thought to be governed by a combination of fluids, or *humours*, within the body. Four humours were recognized: *blood, phlegm, choler* (also called yellow bile), and melancholy (also called *black bile* or *black choler*). The notion transferred readily into a range of senses to do with temperament, mood, inclination, and manner of action (humour (*n.*) 1–4), regarded as permanent or alterable features of behaviour. (2002: 230)

All people were thought to be prone to an excess (slight or otherwise) of one of these humours, which delineated their personality:

> Those inclined towards blood were thought to be ruddy, fair, plump, and of a 'sanguine' or cheerful disposition; those tending towards phlegm of a pale, limp, and languid nature; those prone to black bile of a dark, thin, and melancholic temperament; and those dominated by yellow bile of a fiery, hot-tempered, and choleric character. (Sullivan, 2015: 822)

As Gail Kern Paster writes:

> Like other contemporary playwrights, Shakespeare found in language of the humors and their four qualities of cold, hot, moist, and dry a discourse for signaling the relationship within his characters between embodied emotion and perceptible behaviors, between the mind's inclination and the body's temperature. (2004: 85)

A number of Shakespeare characters are described in the plays with reference to the humours. Multiple characters are referred to as being 'melancholy' – notably Jaques (*AYL*, 2.1.26), Hamlet (*Ham.* 3.1.164) and Don John (*MA*.2.1.5). King Lear (*KL*, 1.1.300), Cassius (*JC*, 4.3.43), Antipholus of Syracuse (*CE*, 2.2.66) and Gloucester (*2HVI*, 1.2.51) are described as 'choleric' Chiron and Demetrius are described by Aaron as 'sanguine' (*TA*, 4.2.99) and Hubert (*KJ*, 2.1.461) as 'this lusty blood' and Mistress Quickly calls Doctor Caius 'phelgmatic' (*MW*, 1.4.69) though she means 'choleric'.

As Robert L. Reid points out, however, and as will be apparent in the first exercise presented here, the humours were not fixed, but formed 'an ever-changing cycle' (1996–7: 147): 'Each person, though of one basic temper, routinely enacts the others according to time of day, of year, of life' (Reid, 1996–7: 147). Where characters are not specifically described as being of a particular character, their humoural composition may be open to interpretation. One might play, in *Twelfth Night* for example, a sanguine, jolly Sir Toby Belch, a languid, phlegmatic one or even one of a melancholic disposition.

Each of the four humours was, in turn, thought to connect to one of the four elements, one of the seasons and one of the times of life:

HUMOUR	PERSONALITY	ELEMENT	SEASON	TIME OF LIFE
Choler	Choleric	Fire	Summer	Childhood
Blood	Sanguine	Air	Spring	Adolescence
Phlegm	Phlegmatic	Water	Autumn	Middle Age
Black Bile	Melancholic	Earth	Winter	Old Age

Indeed, a number of Shakespeare characters are also referred to in terms of their elemental constitution, as a means of describing their personality. Patience in *Henry VIII* is described as 'earthy cold' (4.2.98); Antipholus of Ephesus in *The Comedy of Errors* (4.4.48) and Cornwall in *King Lear* (2.2.281) as 'fiery' and Mistress Ford calls Falstaff a 'watery pumpion' (*MW*, 3.3.36).

This is where Shakespeare's conception of character and emotion and Lecoq's teaching fit neatly together. The four elements are a key part of the Lecoq training. One of the key exercises on the elements comes as part of the exploration of the neutral mask. It also falls under the umbrella of investigations into what Lecoq calls '*identifications*' whereby the student dissolves the boundary between themselves and what they imagine, as in becoming a colour in Chapter 4. In *The Moving Body* Lecoq outlines the work with the four elements under the heading 'Identification with the natural world' (2000: 43). He writes:

I ask each student, with the mask on, to become the different elements of nature: water, fire, air, earth. (2000: 43–4)

In this section, we will lead you through a process of connecting yourself to the four elements one after the other, and then offer up a short analysis of the four key characters in the *Henry IV* plays in relation to humours and elements.

In an article entitled 'Humoral Psychology in Shakespeare's "Henriad"', Reid asserts that 'The Henriad defines the period of Shakespeare's most salient humoralism' (1996–7: 474). He builds on the work of U. C. Knoepflmacher, who argued that the humours constitute the 'symbolic nucleus' (1963: 497–501) of *1 Henry IV*, to associate each of its major characters with one of the humours:

King Henry IV with **melancholy** and **earth**
Prince Hal with **sanguine** and **air.**
Sir Harry Hotspur with **choler** and **fire.**
Sir John Falstaff with **phlegm** and **water.**

As outlined earlier, this is, of course, not the only way to view these characters. Indeed, Prince Hal refers to Falstaff as 'This sanguine coward' (*1H4*, 2.4.235) and Falstaff declares himself to be 'as *melancholy* as a gib cat, or a lugged bear' (*1H4* 1.2.71). The precision of the attributions is less important than their exploration, and we encourage the actor to experiment with more than one humour in relation to each character.

We are going to begin by leading you through a version of each of the four elements before applying them to the four characters from *Henry IV*. You can, of course, follow and apply the exercise to other characters on which you may be working.

The elements in movement

Lecoq liked to approach the element of earth via the tree (Lecoq, 2000: 44).

Earth

- Find a place to stand. Take a few moments to feel your feet in connection to the floor. Stand tall. Feel the space above you and the ground beneath.
- Imagine that there are little shoots coming from the soles of your feet which spread into the ground below. Through the floor, and into the earth somewhere below. Allow those shoots to become roots.

- As the roots become bigger, imagine that they are pulling up nutrients from the earth. The water and sugars from the soil are sucked up through the roots and into your legs, and up to your pelvis and then on up into your body like the trunk of a tree.

- The sap of the tree is rising and fills up your body until you feel your arms rising. Imagine they grow out of you like the branches of a tree.

- Send your attention down to the roots again, to your feet that give you stability. That stability rises up through your trunk into the branches, and out into your fingers, like leaves on the tree. Allow gentle movement in the fingers and arms as if keeping the tree alive. It is being gently blown in the wind.

- Let your arm come down to your sides and feel the urge to move from where you are. Allow it to be game of pulling your feet from the earth. You heave a foot from the ground and reattach it. Do the same with the other.

- Walk through the space. Notice how heavy you are. There is calm, and sureness in your every move.

- Reach down to the earth and imagine picking up a clump of earth in each hand. Take the hands apart and bring your hands with the two bits of mimed clay together. They seem to collide with a perfect gentle clunk. Do this again.

- The next time you bring your hands with the clay together, say out loud, 'what's done, is done,' with the second 'done' coinciding with the clunk of the clay.

- Walk through the space and imagine doing other things, with simplicity, like opening doors, pointing things out and siting down. Do everything with a firm, deliberate quality. It is like the third level of tension but with more weight.

Air

This is an example of how Lecoq would teach the element of air via objects moved by it.

- Take a few moments to just stand in the space. Notice any slight breeze or movement in the air around you.

- Allow yourself to be moved ever so slightly by the air, however small the movement is. Like a whisper, you ease very gracefully and quietly through the space.

- Imagine a paper aeroplane. You throw it and it shoots away from you before soaring upwards, changing direction and spiralling down to the ground.

- Now retrace the flight of this imagined paper dart with your hand and then your whole body. You will need quite a lot of space and if you are doing it together you will need to be careful of one another.

- Imagine a second paper aeroplane. You throw it more gently and drifts away from you and glides peacefully down the ground. Copy the imagined flight of this aeroplane with your whole body too.

- Dart across the space. Run fast but with as little noise as you can.
- Think of a plastic bag caught in the wind. It never gets very far and just gets pushed, pulled, yanked and swirled. Copy that kind of movement with your hand and then follow up by doing it with your whole body.

Water

Lecoq's teaching of water is a prime example of how, in his investigations of identification, there a blurring between the human and the element itself. In this improvisation, you start as a human and become the sea, and then move back to being a human again.

- Imagine you are standing in the sea. It is a warm sea up to your waist. The gentle swell of the water supports you and connects in some way to the water inside you.
- You are further out now with your feet detached from the seabed. The waves are bobbing you up and down and around. There is a mild chaos to how you move.
- The sea becomes rough and you identify with the waves so that you are not so much a person in the sea but partly the sea itself. The movement is jagged, like the tips of waves but smooth at the same time. The water is holding you.
- You are far out at sea now in an increasingly violent storm. Imagine you are raised up enormously and then dumped down into a great trough. You are the sea too.
- You reverse the process until you are back in the calm state of comforting serenity that the warm water gives to you.

There is more water improvisation later in the chapter when you will be introduced to the journey of a river from source to the sea.

Fire

This improvisation can bring up strong emotions and needs to be treated with some care. The image, however, of fire in the belly which it uses is a very useful inspiration for creating an *élan* or impulse for sustaining Shakespeare's long thoughts and rich imagery.

- Find a place to stand and imagine a glowing ember in your stomach. A breeze passes over it and it glows brighter and hotter.

- Place a few imagined twigs on it till it bursts into a little flame or two. Feel the flames light up your chest.

- The fire is bigger now, with small logs to drive it on. The heat increases and fans up into your chest. Surging unpredictably, the fire licks up into your arms, which respond in movement.

- Before long it is like a bonfire and you are forced to move your feet too. The heat is tremendous. You are the fire.

- Cinders spark up and out of you ferociously. Delicate and ferocious at the same time.

- The fire becomes uncontrollable. You begin to move more wildly and your breath is dynamic. As the fire becomes bigger you begin to charge around the space. The fire is monumentally hot now and threatens to consume everything in its path. It is mighty.

- At the same time as you are on fire, you are controlling the experience. You are in between the doer and the done to. It may well be overwhelming. Like level six of tension, you may not be able to withstand it for long.

- Allow breath and voice to ring out, to roar and pierce the sky as you imagine yourself engulfed by the flames and shattering the space around you.

- Start to let the heat decrease. Move around the space more normally. Keep the fire alive inside you but keep your exterior calm. Every so often, the fire bursts out of you in a rapid and unnerving movement. Explore your voice and words with this. Expletives, curses and anger will dominate. Allow this.

- Contain the fire even more. Mime something every day, like dressing yourself or washing, and then let the fire interrupt you. It changes you instantaneously. Keep exploring this shift from control to danger. Gradually, as the fire erupts, you find joy and hilarity in it instead of anger. It is a game, after all.

Connecting humours, Shakespeare and the four elements

We will lead you through a brief exploration of a selection of key characters from *Henry IV* in relation to the elements, air, earth, fire and water, since they each have a specific connection to an element, but you can use the four elements to explore any character.

Sanguine/Air

- Imagine you are playing Hal in *Henry IV, Part 1*. As a very brief introduction, Hal is the heir to the throne and is spending much of his time with a drunken older friend. Hal is stuck between his love of a good time and the impending duty of kingship. He will later become the Henry V of Agincourt fame. The following speech is Hal berating his friend Sir John Falstaff for his lazy ways:

PRINCE
Thou art so fat-witted with drinking of old sack,
and unbuttoning thee after supper, and sleeping upon
benches after noon, that thou hast forgotten to demand that truly
which thou wouldst truly know. What a devil
hast thou to do with the time of the day? Unless hours
were cups of sack, and minutes capons, and clocks the
tongues of bawds, and dials the signs of leaping-houses,
and the blessed sun himself a fair hot wench in flame-coloured
taffeta, I see no reason why thou shouldst be so
superfluous to demand the time of the day. (*1HIV*, 1.2.3-12)

As detailed in Chapter 5, we are going to follow the same principle that Lecoq suggests of seeing the movement work as being 'in relation' to the text (Lecoq, 2000: 146). We are going to explore Hal in relation to the humour type, **sanguine**, which in our terms, is **air**.

- Recap the exploration of **air** from the section 'Air'.
- Go through the speech relatively neutrally, not colouring it with any interpretation, but accompany it with movement

as if being moved by the breeze. It may create a kind of gentleness.

- Now go through the speech again while enacting any number of the paper aeroplanes. You will find hints of Hal's more dynamic nature coming through. He will soar sometimes and plummet at others, amused and then exasperated by Falstaff. Or, if you choose our gliding aeroplane, you might display a calm wisdom beyond Hal's youthful age.

- For a final attempt with this example, go through the speech while under the strain of the flapping and cavorting of the plastic bag in the wind, and it will suggest to you, and those watching, something of the turmoil that is driving Hal.

As discussed earlier, even though **sanguine** may be the key humour for Hal, characters are not exclusively limited to a single humour. It may be useful to explore Hal, and this speech, from the perspective of another humour – **melancholic**, which relates to the element **earth**. Doing this speech in relation to **earth** will give Hal a more rooted, steady energy and might give a feeling of the power and responsibility he will one day inherit from his father.

- As with the tension level explorations of Chapter 4, to start with, infuse the speeches or any improvisation you do with the character, with the element, wholly, without deviating from it.

- Once you have felt how the unilateral choice of the one element informs your characterization then feel free to move on and free things up. All, some or none of what you find with, **air** or **earth** in this instance will stay with you as progress towards performance.

Melancholic/earth

- Imagine you are playing King Henry.
- Explore the character of the King in terms of simple movement, walking through the space, sitting on a throne, getting up from a throne, giving out instruction and so on while channelling the sensations of **earth**, which could

include feeling that you have long roots into the ground, moving as if made of clay, and that you are a tree trunk with branches.

- Explore this speech from the King under the influence of **earth**:

KING
My blood hath been too cold and temperate,
Unapt to stir at these indignities,
And you have found me, for accordingly
You tread upon my patience; but be sure
I will from henceforth rather be myself,
Mighty and to be feared, than my condition,
Which hath been smooth as oil, soft as young down,
And therefore lost that title of respect
Which the proud soul ne'er pays but to the proud.
(1HIV, 1.3.1-9)

- Go through the speech three times with three key aspects: (1) tree roots, (2) clay and (3) the tree's branches.
- Return your awareness to the imaginary roots worming their way into the ground beneath you at the beginning of each verse line, as if filling up on that sense of being grounded.

- Bring your hands, full of clay, together on the last word of each verse line as if marking them as very definite.

- Feel the tall steadiness of the tree's trunk as you speak and on every verse line, bring your arms from your sides slowly up so that, by the last word, they are in the air, like branches. Once you have done that, choose a longer thought and bring the arms up into the branches position more slowly. For instance, in this example, a longer thought could be the whole of the quoted text from 'My blood' to 'the proud'.

- As with Hal, explore the king via **air** too, as a contrast to **earth**. The **earth** for King is what Lecoq might refer to as the mask and **air** for the King is what he might describe as the counter-mask (Lecoq, 2000: 54). The version with **air** may feel less appropriate but could well help to discover an aspect of the king's character beyond his power and solemnity.

Choleric/fire

Our **choleric** example character, Hotspur, is self-evidently under the influence of fire and so a prime candidate for the full **fire** treatment.

- Explore the following speech in relation to the movement of **fire** in the following ways:
- Take a portion of the **fire** exploration that is mentioned earlier and do the whole speech while embodying it. We offer three possible portions:

  a. The heat increases and fans up into your chest. Surging unpredictably.

  b. Cinders spark up and out of you ferociously.

  c. The fire is monumentally hot now and threatens to consume everything in its path. It is mighty.

HOTSPUR
A perilous gash, a very limb lopped off.
And yet, in faith, it is not. His present want
Seems more than we shall find it. Were it good
To set the exact wealth of all our states
All at one cast, to set so rich a main
On the nice hazard of one doubtful hour?
It were not good, for therein should we read
The very bottom and the soul of hope,
The very list, the very utmost bound
Of all our fortunes.

(1HIV, 4.1.43-52)

- Now, contain all that you have experienced with the movements of fire, and speak the speech without moving at all.
- As a complete contrast and as a way of uncovering the counter-mask, play the speech while imaging that you are like the **water** in a bucket that gently sloshes as it is being carried by someone.

Phlegmatic/water

Sir John Falstaff is one of Shakespeare's largest (in every sense) characters. In an act of empathy with his multifarious and overflowing qualities, we are going to expand this exercise to accommodate this huge character. We are going to keep to what was suggested by Reid: that Sir John is **phlegmatic** and, so, connected to **water**. However, we are going to add an additional water exploration from the Lecoq tradition. It is an exercise which Lecoq set while exploring water and it is simply known to us as 'The Journey of a River'. Lecoq explained as he taught this, that this version of a river can be likened to a journey through life.

The journey of a river

The exercise is best done in three stages:

1.   First, have someone read out the description of the river (below) a couple of times while you just listen.

2.   Next have a go at embodying what you have heard with your hand only (you may involve more of your body but the hand is a nice way to make a first approximation of the work).

3.   Finally make an attempt to create a whole physical journey with your whole body as the river. This might take up to about five minutes from spring to the sea.

The fact that much of it is physically out of reach for the human body to actually do is good for activating your physical imagination. As you actually can't be the **rapids** or certainly can't be **the urban river** in the way that we have described it below, you have to find a *transposition*. The attempt to embody these phases of river creates what Lecoq would call a 'poetic body', via rhythms, use of space and gesture. You can only ever do a version of the river, but in your attempt you may land on some kind of essence of it.

We have bolded eight distinct sections of the river so that you and your company will have a recognizable shorthand to use the river while working with it:

- Imagine you are the tiny amount of water surging up from the rocks and trickling out onto the surface of the earth.

- You are now the little rivulet making its way down a very minimal slope. **Spring and trickle.**

- You grow into a small stream. You start to snake your way through the sand, rock and earth, making your way round the vegetation in your way.

- The stream gets bigger and starts to plunge down the side of the hill. Steeper and steeper it becomes, switching this way and that as it pours over and around the rocks. **A mountain stream.**

- The mountain stream plunges meters down and forms a pool. Cold clean water waiting to tumble further down the slope. Many times it happens in falls and pools of different sizes and shapes. **Pools and falls.**

- The stream becomes a river. You are the river. Shallow, widening and passing over more and more smooth pebbles, stones and rocks. The river gets deeper and the rocks become obstacles. The noise is increasing as the water becomes white with a froth as it is impeded. We are in the rapids now. A surging and falling back. Water is flung from bank to bank in an effervescent flurry. **The rapids.**

- In the distance there is roaring sound. The river is deepening and widening. Its enormity is building up in pressure until, eventually, its vastness crashes its enormous volume down the sheer rock face until a hundred meters below it plummets beneath the surface and back up into a huge lagoon. **A waterfall and a lake.**

- Below the lake the river opens up. It is wide and meandering, carving its way through the countryside and agricultural land. There are vessels on the river and people on the banks. This is **the mature river.**

- The river reaches the city. It is boarded by concrete and stone, it is brown with silt and maybe even slightly tidal. It is spanned by impressive bridge and contaminated by debris and even the odd dead body. This is **the urban river.**

- Finally, beyond the city, the river opens up, and there are marshes on either side, sea-birds and waves appear on the water. The horizon becomes huge, and you are not sure if it is a river or the sea. This is **the estuary.**

An example of this exercise can be seen in Video 6: https://bloomsbury.pub/shakespeare-and-lecoq

Falstaff in relation to the river

Falstaff is a character of great range and is thought to be a pinnacle in an actor's career. The Journey of a River, accordingly, has much going on in it, from the sweetness of the **spring and trickle** to the violence of the **rapids** and resignation of the **estuary**.

What links them all is water. They are all ways that water negotiates its journey from when it bubbles to the earth's surface to when it reaches the sea.

In this speech Falstaff is complaining about the people he is forced to work with while simultaneously displaying a begrudging fondness for them.

> FALSTAFF
> I am accursed to rob in that thief's company.
> The rascal hath removed my horse and tied him I know
> not where. If I travel but four foot by the square further
> afoot, I shall break my wind. Well, I doubt not but to
> die a fair death for all this, if I scape hanging for killing
> that rogue. I have forsworn his company hourly any
> time this two-and-twenty years, and yet I am bewitched.
> with the rogue's company. If the rascal have not given
> me medicines to make me love him, I'll be hanged. It
> could not be else: I have drunk medicines . Poins! Hal!
> A plague upon you both! Bardoll! Peto! I'll starve ere
> I'll rob a foot further. An 'twere not as good a deed as drink
> to turn true man and to leave these rogues, I am
> the veriest varlet that ever chewed with a tooth. Eight
> yards of uneven ground is threescore and ten miles
> afoot with me, and the stony-hearted villains know it
> well enough. A plague upon it when thieves cannot be
> true one to another!
>
> (*1HIV*, 2.2.10-27)

- Imagine you are playing Sir John Falstaff.
- Following the principles laid out earlier with the work in **air**, **earth** and **fire**, you are going to improvise with the stages of the Journey of a River. First, look for situations that Sir John finds himself in in the play and then improvise the situation from the standpoint of each of stages of the river (or stages that take your fancy).

- For example, you might undertake an improvisation in which Falstaff is being asked to settle his bar bill – something he is notoriously reluctant to do. The character asking him to settle up stays quite neutral, in level three of tension, and the actor playing Falstaff uses the stages of the river, in succession, to explore the moment. We will make suggestions for the first three:

    a. With **spring and trickle** he will be very muted about the request and maybe finds a moment of deep reflection about his drinking habit in the stillness of it.

    b. In the **mountain stream** mode, he is likely to dance his way around the subject and still not pay up.

    c. In the **pools and falls** movement dynamic, he may seem to be about to pay (the pool) and then falls into another reason for not possibly paying up (the fall).

- Once you have improvised off-script, then try the speech while, at the same time, moving around in different, specific river-like qualities and noticing how the movement brings a new sense of the character that you may not have thought of. Again, we will lay out a few pointers for this particular speech with a reminder that you should try taking on board what we are suggesting and take that forward into your own work. The examples are from the latter part of the river journey. We will assume you have explored the movement dynamics of the river and now, as you speak the speech, allow yourself to have just a trace of what you felt, in movement, to inform your playing choices.

    a. If the speech is done with a trace of the **waterfall and a lake** the actor will be invited to feel a slowly growing pressure from the anger or irritation that Falstaff is feeling and then, at some point, find a massive surge and downpour of energy (the **waterfall** itself) and then a moment, or several moments, of deep release and calm (the **lake**) as a result of doing it.

    It may or may not go with the text but keep to the **waterfall and lake**, come what may, so that you challenge preconceptions about the speech or the moment. This is exploration and the experiments and the text will find a peace with one another in relation to the nature of your company, who you are intending to perform to and of course, your intentions of fidelity or otherwise, to the text itself.

b. When played with a trace of the **mature river**, the character will seem more measured than normal. This could suggest a layer of quiet menace that Sir John may or may not have.

c. The **urban river** will play into what feels embattled, murky and defensive about him.

Leading with different parts of the body

This exercise is an extension of the undulation in Chapter 1. The idea is that we can organize ourselves, as actors, to proceed into the space in front of us with various parts leading or trailing. The reason for leading or trailing with a part of your body might be because of the situation but equally it might be that this has become your character's habit. Much of Lecoq's training was through masks. The mask, almost inevitably, is a type. The half-masks in the second year are taken from the Italian Commedia Dell'Arte.

In the Introduction we discussed the connection between Shakespeare and the Commedia and the way in which some of Shakespeare's characters have a close connection to those of Commedia, either through a direct influence or through their shared origins in the Roman drama of Plautus and Terrence (see Introduction p. 6). Here, the Commedia characters are referenced because each of them has a distinctive body shape which tells the audience something about them before they speak. The characters include Pantalone, the old miser who walks with 'feet together, toes apart, knees well bent and facing apart creating a focus on the crutch' (Rudlin, 1994: 93), Dottore, the pompous windbag whose stance is 'weight back on heels, belly forward' (Rudlin, 1994: 100), and Capitano, the boastful coward whose stance is 'feet planted apart in order to occupy maximum space, chest pushed forward, back straight, hips wide' (Rudlin, 1994: 121). As you can see, each of these characters leads with a different part of their body – Pantalone with his crutch, Dottore with his stomach and Capitano with his chest.

We will lead you through the physical exercise and encourage you to exaggerate all of them to start with and then make them much smaller so that the audience might not see much of a difference from how you might move normally, but the difference is working at a subtle level. Then we will suggest a few possible correlations with Shakespeare characters. They are especially useful if you are doubling or tripling in a production with multiple characters.

Movement exercise

Head

- Start to move through the space but with your head leading. Actually put your head forward as if going through an invisible pane of glass just in front of you. Ask yourself why you might be like this. Are you looking for something? Are you angry? How you experience this will depend, to a large extent, on which part of the head you choose to lead with – the forehead, the nose or the chin.
- As you do the exercise, start to think about characters who might move in this way.

Possible characters: Is your head forward from curiosity, or perhaps from over-thinking? This might be the pedant Holofernes from *Love's Labour's Lost* or a busy, nosey character like Pandarus from *Troilus and Cressida*.

- Now move through the space with your head pulled back. Are you shocked or surprised by something? Scared maybe? Or perhaps you are daydreaming. How does it affect your rhythm?

Possible characters: This could be Juliet dreaming of her Romeo. It might be Miranda in the *Tempest* being taken aback by what she hears from Prospero. It could be any number of the mechanicals in *A Midsummer Night's Dream* who are plunged into the world of dramatics far beyond their capabilities.

Chest

Move through the space with your chest leading. You are likely to feel some pride. Is it a front? Are you covering up for a feeling of inadequacy? Are you simply generous and open?

Possible characters: Is this the military swagger of Don Armado from *Love's Labour's Lost*? Or perhaps the open-hearted romance of Juliet from *Romeo and Juliet*? Could it be the swelling of pride that Othello needs to bring to his first appearance in front of Desdemona's father and the noblemen of Venice?

- Let your chest deflate and make it the last thing to come into the space in front of you. It is as if you are wounded, shy and ashamed maybe.

Possible characters: Is there something about Richard II that knows he is defeated from the outset? Could this be Dromio of Ephesus from *A Comedy of Errors* whose chest is giving in to the doubts and the possible next beating from his master, Antipholus?

Pelvis

- Bring your pelvis forward. With this you allow your stomach to protrude. Do this with relaxation and you might feel a connection to your mouth. The mouth and belly are linked. Do you feel a tingle of sensuousness? Greed? Is the appetite whetted by allowing the belly to enter the space first? Your genitals are also here. Is there a kind of freedom in exposing that part of yourself?

Possible characters: This is very possibly Falstaff (*HIV 1* and *2* and *The Merry Wives of Windsor*) with his vast appetite preceding him. It might equally be Mistress Overdone, the bawd from *Measure for Measure*.

- Now suck the belly and genitals back as if to hide them from the space. See how that affects you. Like all of these, there will be variations but it is broadly predictable that bringing your pelvis back will make you feel more cautious, more precise even, more contained.

Possible characters: Perhaps this is the novice nun Isabella from *Measure for Measure*. It might equally be her would-be seductor Angelo, desperately trying to deny his sexual urges.

Feet and knees

- The last of the focal points in the undulation is the knees and for this, you can consider how it is to have your knees and feet go before you. It may feel a bit comic, almost like a clown's oversized feet. It may be the result of creeping quietly and having to mind your step.

Possible characters: A character who 'puts their foot in it' like a Bottom or Dogberry from *Much Ado* might channel this. Less idiotically, perhaps Shylock in *The Merchant of Venice* might proceed foot first as someone who needs to be wary of those around him and may have developed, in one side of his character, the ability to tread carefully.

- If your knees and feet are the last things to enter the space you will feel off-balance. You will totter somewhat. It might feel funny, as if you are not able to support yourself.

Possible characters: This could be useful in a comic character who is running ahead of themselves like Grumio, Petruchio's servant in *Taming of the Shrew*, or more tragically, Ophelia, whose life in *Hamlet* is running away from her.

Each of these leading body part investigations is a starting point for an exploration of rhythm, breath, 'size' and *attitude* of the character. It is vital to have the character live as a physical entity clearly before even any words are said. These explorations might lead to a particular body language or gait, or they might be brought back to what Lecoq calls the level of 'respiration, in apparent immobility' (2000: 79), by which he means near stillness and available for subtle play if needed.

Exploring the dramatic dynamism of pushing and pulling

Action mime shows us that everything a person does in their life can be reduced to two essential actions: 'to pull' and 'to push'. We do nothing else! (Lecoq, 2000: 85–6)

This is a great example of how Lecoq's teaching sought to essentialize experience into readily feelable, kinetic, notions. In this section, therefore, we will unveil Lecoq's procedures around pushing and pulling and offer some relationships to a Shakespeare speech.

Pushing and pulling each other/yourself

As Lecoq explains in *The Moving Body*, the actions of 'to pull' and 'to push' 'include the passive "I am pulled" and "I am pushed" and the reflexive "I pull myself" and "I push myself" and can go in many different directions: forwards, to one side or the other, backwards, diagonally, etc. I call this the rose of effort' (2000: 86).

Pushing

- Find a partner of roughly similar size, and agree who is to push and who is to be pushed. A (pushing) and B (pushed).
- B stands tall, ready to gently resist A. A put their palms on the area at the top of B's torso near their shoulders. A pushes B. Make it a game, so proceed with lightness but make sure that A gets to experience some of the struggle and high tension of pushing and B gets to feel the pleasure of resisting and being budged and maybe even transported a short distance by A.
- Swap over so B gets to push A.

Pulling

- Swap again but this time A will pull B. B holds out their arms and A holds them and leans back and pulls B forwards.

- Swap roles so that B pulls A.
- B then stands with their back to A, and A wraps their arms around B's waist as B attempts to locomote forwards with B hanging on to them.
- Change roles.

Pushing and pulling yourself

- Think about the expression, 'pushing yourself' and see what happens if you try it out in the space. It is like pushing but is a bit more complex, as if there is some resistance.
- Think about the expression, 'pulling yourself up' and see what happens. Again, it is similar to pulling in some aspects but there is touch more struggle involved.

Connecting to Shakespeare (using the push/pull to reveal character)

To make these effort movements more appreciable in relation to Shakespeare, you are going to begin by moving through the space exploring each of the six basic variations that Lecoq suggests and noticing how they affect your inner space, or your emotional and psychological response.

It is useful in this exercise to use Lecoq's maxim of expanding movement 'to its maximum' and then reducing it down 'to the point where it is almost imperceptible from outside' (2000: 78–9). Begin by doing each of these movements to the maximum (using a partner, if necessary, to summon the feeling of being pushed or pulled). As you reduce the movement down, become aware of how it feels to walk through the space with the feeling of pushing, pulling, being pushed, being pulled, pushing yourself or pulling yourself. We will give just one example per action, but, as ever, there are many more. You may resonate with ours, but please find alternatives.

- **Push.** Might summon *determination*.
- **Pull.** Could create a feeling of *enthusiasm*.
- **Being pushed.** Will bring up a *reluctance*.

- **Being pulled.** Might involve a *seduction*.
- **I push myself.** Calls forth *urgency*.
- **I pull myself.** Might summon *hope*.
- Take a speech from the play you are working on and treat it in succession with the dynamics of the pushing and pulling experiments and see what it reveals to you and the ensemble about the character.

We will now take a short speech from *Henry VIII* where Queen Katherine is making a suit to King Henry on behalf of the people as an example of the sorts of benefits you can get from this process.

> QUEEN KATHERINE
> I am solicited, not by a few,
> And those of true condition, that your subjects
> Are in great grievance: there have been commissions
> Sent down among 'em, which hath flaw's the heart
> Of all their loyalties
>
> *(H8, 1.2.18-22)*

- Imagine you are playing Queen Katherine. You are going to apply what you have just learned from 'pushing' and 'pulling' through the space to this speech.

As with the four elements, in the first section of this chapter, your way of using the physical movement can be on a scale. You may want to try the speech in three levels:

1. Fully miming pushing or pulling an object at the same time;

2. Walking while speaking and feeling like you are pushing, pulling, being pushed, pulled or pushing or pulling yourself which would mean, at this level, the walk having a particular kind of energy;

3. Reducing the activity more, you can say the lines almost just thinking about the particular version of push/pull (once you have experienced the movement version first).

- Say the lines while **pushing** at all three levels (1) fully miming **pushing** something, (2) walking as if **pushing** through the space and (3) simply thinking about **pushing**. The results of this may be that Queen Katherine's sense of *determination* becomes highlighted and her political credentials established.

- Say the lines while **pulling** at all three levels. Queen Katherine may become *more girlish* as she finds a way to start her appeal to the king.

- Say the lines while **being pushed** at all three levels (if you need to use a partner for the first version to summon this feeling, then do so). Katherine's *duty towards her king* might come into focus, as she has a divided loyalty, among other things.

- Say the lines while **being pulled** at all three levels (with or without a partner). Maybe Katherine's *desire and love* for Henry play a bigger part. It might only be felt by the actor playing the King but it is there.

- Say the lines while imagining the dynamics of **pushing yourself,** at all three levels and you may find that she is almost *overcome by a rush of impulse* to say what she has to say.

- Finally say the lines while imagining the dynamics of **pulling yourself** at all three levels and the delivery has an air of *lightness, hope and expectation.*

As you will have noticed if you were to take this exercise completely as we have laid it out, you will have done the speech eighteen times! We are simply laying out all the possibilities for you to choose from. It may be that you are working on a speech from Dogberry in *Much Ado About Nothing,* and you just think about doing it with a sense of **being pulled** and your speech, the moment and character all become clear to you. Our intention is for you to take inspiration from what we are offering. The beauty of this approach is that you are availing yourself of many playing choices with a tangible physical process which will not only motivate you, but will be felt by the other actor and will even be detected at some level by the audience.

7

Exploring character drives

Of character, Lecoq says the following:

> When we begin the work on characters, I am always afraid the students will fall back on personality, in other words talk about themselves, with no element of genuine play. If character becomes identical with personality, there is no play. It may be possible for this kind of osmosis to work in the cinema, in psychological closeups, but theatre performance must be able to make an image carry from stage to spectator. There is a huge difference between actors who express their own lives, and those who can truly be described as players. (2000: 61)

As can be seen from this assertion, Lecoq rejected forms of acting in which the actor sought to identify entirely with the character – to 'become' the character. Indeed, the Lecoq school leads students away from any form of psychological interpretation of character as advocated by practitioners such as Stanislavsky. Such a rejection of ultra-naturalism seems appropriate when tackling Shakespeare's characters. Many of the conventions of the early modern theatre were inherently non-naturalistic, from boys playing female characters to characters directly addressing the audience, and characters speaking in verse. Shakespeare's plays also have a heightened quality. As Katherine A. Craik asserts, 'few would dispute that emotional intensity is the hallmark of Shakespearean drama' (2020: 1).

In the last chapter we looked at broad character types. In this chapter we home in on character detailing. In doing so, we encourage the actor to use Lecoq's methods to find the size and range of their

Shakespearean character(s) to embrace the heightened language and emotions present in the plays.

We begin by introducing you to a strategy of Lecoq's to particularize your stage presence to suit the character you are playing – establishing their 'characteristics' or the 'lines of force which define' them (Lecoq, 2000: 64). Following this work, we will dip into the vast world of animal *mimage* that Shakespeare's text suggest, making use of Lecoq's work on 'studying animals' as a means of 'character creation' (Lecoq, 2000: 92). Finally, we will move on to 'passions' – a word used in the early modern period to define what are now more commonly thought of as 'emotions'. 'Passions' is also a term used frequently by Lecoq with reference to a character's driving force.

Three words for characteristics

Lecoq's approach to character

In *The Moving Body* Lecoq alludes to the process by which he invites his students to create what he calls *personnages*, or characters, by suggesting that the first thing to do when creating a character is to define their characteristics, or in more colloquial form, what they are like. Lecoq uses a very specific phrase to say this. He calls these characteristics 'the lines of force which define it' (2000: 64). He adds:

> their definition must be reducible to three words. A given character might be: 'proud, generous and quick-tempered'. In this way we simplify the definition as far as possible in order to establish the basic structure which will permit the actor to play the character. (2000: 64)

First, we will look at an example of a Shakespeare character, Trinculo, from *The Tempest*, giving them three basic characteristics, to give you some guidance before you break down your own character in this way. Then we will come to what makes Lecoq's version of characterizing so special by going back to the phrase: 'lines of force which define it'.

- Choose a character that you are playing or preparing for and, without thinking too hard about it, to come up with three key characteristics for them.

This, for example, is how Kenneth McLeish and Stephen Unwin describe Trinculo from *The Tempest:*

> Drink makes Caliban pugnacious and Stephano pompous, and it makes Alonso's jester [Trinculo] melancholy. He spends the play following his companions through horseponds and middens on their farcical quest to overthrow Prospero and make Stephano king in his place. Even so, and for all his drunken grumbling, enough shreds of sharp-tongued wit remain to remind us of his former profession – 'The folly of the island! They say there's but five upon this isle. We are three of them. I th'other two be brain'd like us, the state totters'. (1998: 201)

From this description we can extract **lugubrious, complaining** and **waspish,** three contrasting descriptors. Lecoq said that 'lines of force' define the character and so we will now investigate space, shape, force, rhythm in relation to these three words for Trinculo.

Embodying characteristics and creating a character sequence

- Find a space to work in. Think of the first word you have chosen, in this case, **lugubrious.**
- Just let it work on you in some way. *It might make you feel different.*
- Start to move through the space in a lugubrious way. This will be heavy, downcast maybe, with sways from side to side.
- Get to a point where you exaggerate the lugubriousness until it feels like it becomes very 'over-acted' and then shift the movement into something that feels more dance-like or abstract.
- Keep moving in this way until you identify three main branches of movement. For example, with **lugubrious,** it might be that

  1. the sway from side to side (see above) turns into a pendulum type movement with arms shooting out on each side;
  2. you discover a forwards and backwards shuffling type of move;
  3. you develop a sort of slow spinning on the spot.

- Once you have identified the three movements take a couple of minutes to confirm them to yourself and find a way that you are likely to remember them. You could use a phone camera, write it down or draw something. This is your first movement sequence.

- Repeat this process of making a sequence for the next two words, **complaining** and **waspish**.

- Once you have three movements, linked into a movement sequence for each of the three words, recap all of these. You will then have a sequence of nine movements. If you have done your job effectively, you will have a kind of movement version of the character that can be repeated and practiced at various points in rehearsal to help you find the essence of your character.

- If you are working in an ensemble, show each other the movements, and you will be inspired and motivated by how clearly the others can read your character even as it is in semi-abstract movement. You and the ensemble will learn much about the characters from this process: information that was lying at a bodily level.

- Bring those movements to their maximum, before reducing them to the level of respiration and apparent stillness as described by Lecoq (2000: 78–9). This will ensure that you are flexible in your ability to use the sequence.

You now have a version of the three words for the character as treated physically in terms of 'lines of force that define' them (2000: 64). This sequence is very much a starting point and will lend you a living, breathing, dynamic template from which to develop the character. It will help to embody your character choices.

Exploring character through animals

thou art the thing itself.
Unaccommodated man is no more but such a poor,
bare, forked animal as thou art.

(KL, 3.4.104-6)

Shakespeare's plays teem with animal imagery. The variety is astonishing, as Laurie Shannon points out in her paper 'The Eight Animals in Shakespeare; Or, Before the Human', listing some of the animals mentioned in the plays:

> the winter lion, the Hyrcanian tiger, and baited bear; the little shrew and the necessary cat; bottled spiders and horned toads; brave harts and gentle hinds; the forward horse and preposterous ass; the temple-haunting martlet, morning lark, nightly owl and winging crow; the nibbling sheep and hunger-starved wolves; the chafed boar, princely palfrey, fat oxen, and spotted leopards; stranger curs mastiffs, hellhounds. (Shannon, 2009: 473–4)

Actors have often used animal imagery and movement when exploring Shakespeare's characters in rehearsal and performance. Actor Antony Sher famously used the image of a 'bottled spider' to create a monstrous multi-limbed creature for his famous *Richard III* (see Sher, 1985). A more Lecoq-related animal transformation is recorded by Helen Richardson, who tells the story of how, for the 2013–15 performance of *Macbeth* by the Théâtre du Soleil, actor Serge Nicolaï, studied the

> physicality of an ape to render the character of Macbeth, suggesting a man who is aping a ruler who is pushed by instinct to pursue power without the moral conscience necessary to regulate his own actions. Nicolaï would dangles his arms and look about, unsure of his next action, projecting a vacant expression and body poised for violence as his instincts dominated his capacity for thought. (2016: 310)

What is strong about using the ape to get into Macbeth is partly how it seems right and wrong at the same time. When actors train in drama schools there is often an animal studies component, and in opening up the student actor to new possibilities in their approach, teachers will often select an animal for the student which suits them ('right') and one which challenges them ('wrong'). Lecoq did not dictate the animal choice to his students but did encourage them to find, through observation, ideally at the zoo or in the wild, two contrasting animals to create a dynamic range between differing energies.

Many of Lecoq's training methods can be traced back to Jacques Copeau and Suzanne Bing at the Théâtre du Vieux-Colombier. Bing is credited with bringing animal studies into the training at the Vieux-Colombier. As Mark Evans explains:

Animal work offered the opportunity to develop several important aspects of the School's pedagogy at the same time: examination of the dynamics of the natural world; challenging of the student's imaginative resources; exploration of the potential for self-transformation; development of the student's physical skills and control; and, subversion of the inhibiting influence of the intellect. (2006: 131)

Lecoq, naturally, subscribed to all of these, and it is perhaps the last of these examples from the list which is most pertinent here, as it is the intellect which is so easily seduced by Shakespeare's complexity and literary history.

Animal study exercise

There is no manual to Lecoq's approach to animal studies. He refers to it engagingly but in broad strokes in *The Moving Body* (2000: 92). He does, however, make it clear that, although the animals that the students observe, either in the zoo or the wild, or on video, are to be imitated, to a degree, it is not an attempt to 'perform exceptional feats, but rather to discover the elementary, organic movements of the animals' (Lecoq, 2000: 93). There is no limit to what you might study but let's take a couple of examples from Laurie Shannon's list to give you a flavour of how some of the animals mentioned in Shakespeare might inspire your transformations into character:

> the little shrew
>
> hunger-starved wolves

- Make sure you have clothes that are comfortable to move in and if you are thinking of being on all fours, it would be sensible to have some knee pads and mats available for your preliminary explorations.

- The common shrew is a small rodent which could be mistaken for a rat from a distance. It has a compact, furred body with a furless tail. It has a protuberant nose which twitches around to detect its insect prey. It runs a very high metabolism, which means it only lives for a year. It nozzles around in undergrowth, stopping and starting and switching directions with alacrity. It also emits a high-pitched sound almost inaudible to the human ear.

- Take your time to find as accurate a version of its body as you can. You will be curled up to a degree and you may try a version of the animal on all fours. It has very small eyes, and so uses its muzzle to navigate. You can mimic this with your whole face. You can imagine the tail whipping around behind you, keeping you balanced. It has a quick and jerky rhythm suggesting, if we anthropomorphize it, a kind of nervousness. You may wish to explore a very faint high-pitched sound.

- Possible characters to take this animal into include Polonius from *Hamlet*, Justice Shallow from *Henry IV*, Part 2, and the Nurse from *Romeo and Juliet*.

- Wolves are not kept in zoos but can be seen in controlled parks, and of course, on film. Another four-legged creature but this time with great stamina and range. It is of course, the progenitor of our domesticated dogs and has many similar qualities to the Alsatian or Huskey but it is a predator and so uses its nose in a different way. It can often be seen with its muzzle to the ground but its eyes scanning the horizon. Its movement might at times be described as rather rangey compared to the dogs we are familiar with. It is famous, of course, for its howling and so this is an interesting aspect of the wolf to try and emulate both as a movement and as a sound. Imitate as much of this as you can on all fours and then take it into standing as Mark Evans, Lecoq and Copeau expert, describes below.

- Possible characters to take this animal into include Claudius from *Hamlet*, Lady Macbeth from *Macbeth* and Don John from *Much Ado About Nothing*.

Develop the animal you have worked on into a human character. Begin by improvising as the animal, and then gradually start to develop towards a human representation. As far as is possible, within a human frame, maintain the animal's sense of weight, rhythm, posture, breath, focus, and need. Think of your creation as half-human and half-animal. Now explore this character's movement, posture, interaction, voice, social status and use of space. (Evans, 2006: 134)

This 'half-human and half-animal' state is a very powerful one to rehearse in as it helps to push your choices to extremes. Please consider finding this half-way-house as you attempt the next exercises with your own characters.

Connecting to Shakespeare (using animals to inform character)

Let's take Goneril from *King Lear* as an example of how to infiltrate the process of preparing Shakespeare with animals. You may even find in your reading of the text that the character you are playing is referred to as animal and so that is a good place to start, but if they are not, then find one that you feel is suited to the character.

- Goneril is referred to as a kite, a vicious bird of prey:

LEAR. [*to Goneril*]
Detested kite, thou liest.

(KL, 1.4.254)

This is an insult from her father and may well be of use in finding her character. A kite soars and waits before it goes in for the kill. Lecoq does offer a lovely image of how to use animals even if his book is more inspiration than manual: 'A man searching through papers, for example, will begin to show the mouse which is latent within him' (2000: 46). Let's use this to uncover the bird of prey at the heart of Goneril.

- First, take the time you need to study and copy the kite as fully as possible in the way we have described above.
- When the kite is firmly imprinted in your body, then start to do some improvisations, for example, simple activities from Goneril's domestic life.
- Find several differing activities. It could be as simple as

1. dictating orders to her people,
2. tidying her room,
3. negotiating something with her husband.

These can be done with other company members, or on your own, imagining other characters.

- Once you are confident with the basic activities which might or might not contain language, find a moment in the action of what you are doing to be taken over by the movement of the bird. Imagine that, in that moment you

    1. grow wings,
    2. articulate your head in a bird-like fashion, or
    3. swoop on an object or person in a way much more animal than human.

- You will find that this 'subversion of the intellect' (Evans, 2006: 131) will be remarkably freeing and that, you will start to play scenes as Goneril in a way that is much more in tune with what Lecoq and many other educators are hoping for, that 'there should be no sense of the body "getting in the way"'. (Lecoq, 2000: 70)

Animal 2 or counter-mask

Even though Shakespeare's characters speak their minds and the plays do not have what has become known as 'subtext' in modern plays, the characters still have many layers, and often have a front which is contradicted by another side of them. At the school, Lecoq explored this via what he called the 'counter-mask' (2000: 54). So, if for instance, an actor is playing in a mask, that is, 'foolish, timid and clumsy', they will then be asked to consider

what if the character might be knowledgeable, clever, sure of himself, supremely intelligent? (Lecoq, 2000: 61)

In any of Shakespeare's characters, especially the great ones, there is ample opportunity to play on multiple levels, finding at least a mask and counter-mask and maybe more still. We should be clear that this work can be done without the use of actual masks – conceiving the 'mask' as the surface character and the 'counter-mask' as what lies behind it.

For our purposes here, of integrating animal studies, we are simply going to apply the choice of another animal to the exploration of Goneril's character.

- Choose a completely different animal – a crocodile. It is cumbersome on land, at least, and has a huge, obvious and ferocious killer mouth.

- Go through the animal preparation exercises using the crocodile. Then re-do the exercise of going about your business as Goneril in improvisation.

- This time you will choose a moment (or moments), when your activity suggests it, to turn into the crocodile, for example:

  1. when alone, not being judged, feeling like you can walk more cumbersomely,
  2. being openly threatening towards a servant,
  3. devouring your husband with your enormous mouth.

Taking the animals into scenes: Solo

The following is an example of what Lecoq would call a *basculation,* or a reversal of fortunes, a favourite ingredient of many improvisations. It inspires an *auto-cours* at the school, where the group all starts a scenario in one animal and end in another. The content of the situation has converted them.

- This can be done while improvising off-script or when you have learnt the lines.

- Rehearse or improvise a scene by starting as the crocodile and ending as the kite. You may play with how gradually you change but, as an exercise, put the changing of the animal quality before anything else.

- Reverse this so you rehearse the scene again but this time starting as kite and ending as the crocodile.

- Rehearse the scene a third time and this time let yourself flip from one animal whenever it seems right but make sure you are in one of the animals at any given moment.

Taking the animals into scenes: Pair work

- Imagine, now, you are working on a scene with Goneril and her sister Regan.
- Choose two contrasting animals for Regan. Let's say the tiger and wild boar, both of which have a starting point in the text itself – Gloucester referring to both sisters as having 'boarish fangs' (3.7.57) and Albany describing them as 'tigers not daughters' (4.2.41).
- Work through the stages of preparation from above to find the qualities of the two animals.
- Then play the scene. Each of the actors starts the scene in one animal and ends in the other. Reverse it and as before, do a third round where the actors are free to change animal multiple times in the scene.

Exploring passions

Lecoq processed the world around him in terms of movement. In effect, what the training is designed to do is to get theatre-makers to think in movement terms. It could be argued, as we have suggested earlier, that this thinking in terms of movement might be better understood by the early modern era than by the modern actor. Indeed, this is what Evelyn Tribble proposes in her book *Early Modern Actors and Shakespeare's Theatre: Thinking with the Body*. Movement director Ayse Tashkiran, who has worked with the RSC as well as training a new generation of movement directors, goes as far as to say, 'Shakespeare writes the body. Cosmology and the human body reflect one another. . . . In Shakespeare's world "downhearted" is more than a metaphor and for Lecoq-trained movement directors this is concrete, not abstract' (Tashkiran, 2022).

Bridget Escolme explains that to Shakespeare's contemporaries movement was profoundly linked to feeling. The term 'moved' in the early modern period was 'much more active' – 'it can contain the same sense of compassionate feeling but usually results in someone being moved to do something' (2013: xxii). As Escolme also explains, the word 'emotion' would not have been used by the early moderns in the way that we use it today – the 'common equivalent term' being 'passion' (2013: xix), a word closely aligned to Lecoq's own teaching (Lecoq, 2000: 63).

Shakespeare would have inherited his ideas about 'passions' from Cicero, who identified four, which he defined as pleasure, pain, desire and fear and from Thomas Aquinas, who identified eleven fundamental passions: **love, hate, desire, aversion, joy, sorrow, hope, despair, confidence, fear** and **anger** (Roach, 1993: 26, 31). As Mnouchkine writes: 'Shakespeare is extremely versatile in terms of passions; there can be a consuming fury in one half of a line and blissful euphoria in the next' (Williams, 1998: 119).

What follows is an exercise in finding the movement of the passions, to enable you to achieve more easily the bringing of states or passions to the stage. We are using the word 'pot' as a way of encouraging the notion that your movement explorations in passions can be contained to be used and deployed when needed, as if opening up a pot of paint.

Passion pots

The overall aim of this is to take each of the eleven passions of Aquinas, and move simply, to embody them, to start with. Exaggerate the movement as Lecoq has suggested. And use the exaggeration to feel that you are allowing the passion to take you over more and more. Go so far with it that you actually feel that you are being led to a kind of insanity. Bridget Escolme explains how passions of the early modern period were believed to be the thin end of the wedge towards madness:

> The passions are material forces barely under the control of what really makes man human: his sovereign reason [. . .] – anger laughter love and grief – often appear to the early modern philosophical mindset to sit along a continuum at the far end of which is madness. Anger is a potentially murderous mania; the mad laugh unpredictably and inappropriately; love leads to the sickness of 'love melancholy'; grief is the prime producer of melancholic insanity. (2013: vix)

We will not go through all of them, but it will help us to detail one to give you a lead. **Confidence** is on the list of Aquinas' eleven.

Confidence as a passion

- First, just walk through the space with **confidence**. You can simply think of it. Notice changes of rhythm, breath and gaze. Stay with this for a minute or two.

- Then start to allow your hands and arms to do something to do with **confidence**, which might be firming up the hands into a soft fist and bringing the arms out in front. You might pump your hands and arms.

- Include the legs in your exploration of **confidence**. One leg might twist around the other in a kind of spin.

- You may hop, skip or even jump.

Towards the madness of confidence

- The hands start to scrunch in and out.

- The arms pump faster.

- The legs do a dance which gets in a tangle.

- You jump very high, and then lie on your back without a care that any harm can ever come to you.

Adding voice

- See if you can replicate any or all of the movements from the confidence passion pot with sound.

- Have fun distinguishing between the sound of 'jumping high' and 'lying on the floor', or finding the difference between the sound equivalent of your legs twisting round each other and the madder version of the legs getting out of control. Don't get stuck on being able to get it right. There really is no right here. The attempt to push yourself into unusual territory is enough at the moment.

- Now go back to just walking through the space but remember all the things that **confidence** might make you do if it was in charge, and because, it was thought that passions constituted the overthrow of reason in Shakespeare's day, allow yourself to run the gamut from socially acceptable confidence moves, all the way to the outlandish and almost out of control moves.

- Do the same for all of the other ten passions and you will have a rich tool bag of potential states that can be drawn upon to help you rise to the challenge of Shakespeare's heightened poetic world.

Connecting to Shakespeare (playing the rhythm)

The key difference here between the movement sequences for character, earlier in the chapter and these passion pots, is that the passion pots are to encourage you to show the audience, from the moment you enter, what it is that is driving you. The exercise derives from Lecoq's teaching and the Commedia dell'Arte, where the masked character has no past and no future and is entirely in the moment. In that moment, they show, in some ways, all that they are.

- Arrange yourselves as an audience and have someone hold a stick vertically. Delineate with chairs or tape on the floor where the actor crosses onto the 'stage'. The point is that when they are on stage, they play the rhythm of the passion of the character.

- Ask an actor who has prepared a suitable passion for their character in the way that we have instructed earlier. This could be one of our eleven, but there are others – Cicero's four: pleasure, pain, desire and fear, and if we follow Mnouchkine's logic, it is almost anything you feel you want to communicate to the audience.

- Consider the character's first entrance. Even if they would enter with others in the play, for this exercise, they are isolated for clarity's sake.

- The person controlling the stick bangs it on the floor three times (a tradition at the Comédie Française before a play, which Lecoq liked to use in this exercise) to indicate that the actor should 'enter' to improvise. All they have, however, is their passion.

- Their passion must live in movement. It must be sustained by rhythm. It is not a matter of emoting or hiding one's feelings. As Mnouchkine says:

I often have the feeling that people content themselves today with 'performing the words'. In our work what we call the 'state' is the primary passion which preoccupies the actor. So when he is 'angry' he must *draw* the anger, he must *act*. (Williams, 1998: 96)

- This will be difficult and you will be faced with the dilemma of not knowing what to do, and how to find the line between demonstrating and embodying, and playing and pushing, acting and performing. We cannot solve those things for you in this book. It is for you to try the work and see how it lands in your ensemble.

Here is an example from *Twelfth Night* to give you an insight. The actor playing Orsino is playing the game. The stick bangs three times, and he comes on stage. His passion is **love**. Is it in his walk? Is it in his eyes? Does his breathing contain it? Can it be sustained without saying the words? Does it exist at a rhythmical level? Lecoq or his follower, Gaulier, would have no hesitation in crying out 'stop' if the passion was not being played. Mnouchkine, the most prolific of Lecoq's high-profile graduates in producing Shakespeare, says that you must not come on stage with an idea but that 'To enter on to a stage, is to enter into a symbolic place where everything is musical and poetic' (Williams, 1998: 166). The playing of the passion needs to attain to the quality of music.

Here is a final example from *Hamlet*. The actor playing Polonius is doing the exercise. Three taps from the stick, which raises the stakes for the improvisation, and they must come on stage with their chosen passion. It could well be **hope**. Is it present in their whole body? Is it in their eyes? Is the rhythm there? If it is present then the spoken lines will be more likely to float out with 'smoothness' filled with energy of passion that has given birth to it: 'Yet here, Laertes? Aboard, aboard for shame!' (1.3.54).

As you do this exercise, imagine rising to this challenging statement by Mnouchkine: 'Shakespeare's characters often contemplate their interior landscapes. The passion they feel must be translated by the actor. There is a chemistry. It isn't only a question of feeling, it's a question of showing' (Williams, 1998: 96).

8

Exploring clowning and fooling

Perhaps one of the most obvious areas in which the work of Shakespeare and the work of Lecoq might be seen to overlap is that of clowning. Clowning has become a particularly well-known part of the Lecoq training. As this chapter will discuss, there is some natural affinity between Lecoq's clowning work and some of Shakespeare's comic characters. However, the wide range of clown and fool characters in Shakespeare invites further interrogation and benefits from the introduction of another part of the Lecoq training – the *bouffon*.

When Shakespeare's plays were published in the First Folio in 1623, they were divided into comedies, histories and tragedies. Since this time various other categories have been proposed to better define and group the broad cannon, including 'problem-plays', 'romances' and 'late plays'. Irrespective of genre, a number of these plays contain characters who are defined as clowns or fools. These titles are often used interchangeably, but it is generally accepted that the characters fall into two broad categories – the 'natural' clown – a simple, witless figure, such as Bottom in *A Midsummer Night's Dream*, Dogberry in *Much Ado*, Costard in *Love's Labour's Lost*, The Gravediggers in *Hamlet* and Launcelot Gobbo in *Merchant of Venice*, and the professional fool – Feste in *Twelfth Night*, Touchstone in *As You Like It*, Lavache in *All's Well That Ends Well* and Lear's Fool in *King Lear*. The clowns engage in foolish behaviour, often involving physical humour and misuse of language. The professional fools are akin to jesters, who were a common feature of the Renaissance household and court – not only providing entertainment but also meting out criticism to their social superiors under the guise of folly. As Muriel Bradbrook notes, these characters tend to be more fully integrated into the action of the plays, interacting with the central characters and the main plot, providing more than simply distracting humour.

Sara Romersberger, one of the few people to have written about the parallels between Shakespeare's clowns and Lecoq's clowns, asserts:

> Shakespeare's clowns, like Lecoq's personal clowns, have frailties, strengths, successes, and failures. . . . Even in ridiculous situations, their reactions had to be profoundly human and plausible for their characters. . . . Whether for rustic or witty fool, Shakespeare wrote text or created moments that implied fragility and sensitivity for his clowns. (2016: 174–5)

We are going to suggest that Shakespeare's 'natural' clown has a strong affinity with Lecoq's clown, while Shakespeare's professional fool might share more qualities with Lecoq's *bouffon*. Lecoq draws a useful distinction between the clown and the *bouffon,* asserting, 'while we make fun of the clown, the bouffon makes fun of us' (2006: 118). Clowning comes very near the end of the Lecoq training and encourages, among other things, the students to find openness and vulnerability. *Bouffon,* on the other hand, comes in the middle of the second year, alongside tragedy and has been referred to as the 'a tragic clown' (Mason, 2016: 159). *Bouffons* were described by Lecoq as 'people who believe in nothing and make fun of everything' (2000: 124). As Bim Mason elucidates: 'They do so from the perspective of outsiders, rejects or eccentrics, fearful of physical persecution but with no respect for established authority, ideology or the divine' (2016: 157). Like the professional fool of the early modern period, the *bouffon* exists outside of the rigid structures of society. Both are charged with a duty to play and reveal truths that ordinary people, be they kings, queens or commoners, cannot see:

> Bouffons belong to the realm of madness, to that madness which you need the better to safeguard truth. One accepts in a madman what one wouldn't accept in a so-called normal

person. One forgives him when he says upsetting things but one listens to him as a king listens to his fool. (Lecoq, 2000: 119–120)

In this chapter, we will offer up some clown and *bouffon* exercises to help you approach Shakespeare's simple clowns and professional fools. We also suggest that exercises in both clown and *bouffon* might be applied to some of Shakespeare's more serious, and even tragic, characters.

The clown

The Lecoq clown training seeks to tap into every student's inherent foolishness, or stupidity, which they would normally keep hidden from others and bring it out into the open to celebrate it. The clown is not a character and not acted. It is a version of yourself, unveiled in relation to the audience. It is not played *for* an audience but explored *with* an audience. The games and exercise here can be played while wearing a little plastic red nose with an elastic strap, or what Lecoq called 'the smallest mask in the world' (2000: 154). If you and your group have these, then use them, but if not, all of these exercises can be done without. Ideally, the actor reveals weaknesses in discovering their clown, which can be unsettling, but, as Lecoq made clear: 'In fact the clown should never be hurtful for the actor. The audience does not directly make fun of him; they feel superior and laugh which is very different' (2000: 159).

Dressing up

One of the challenges of Shakespeare for contemporary actors and companies is that it can be daunting because of the history of the plays, the reverence for the language (especially for English-speaking companies) and the complexity of the stories. We will now propose an exercise to fast-track a sense of fun and abandon inspired by Lecoq:

You are to put on a disguise, as if you were going to a fancy-dress party. A trunk is brought in with all kinds of props and costumes.

Everyone puts on a false beard or moustache or a funny hat and enjoys themselves in total freedom. (Lecoq, 2000: 156)

For this exercise, you will need a pile of coats, trousers and hats that are out of fashion, too big, too small. You might bring them from home, from a car boot sale or costume store. They should be clothes that you would be unlikely to wear in your normal life.

Finding your clothes

- Take a few minutes to cobble together some unlikely collision of clothes to wear. Put together a mishappen or unusual outfit from the disparate clothing.

Move through the space and notice what comes naturally to you in relation to the clothes you have chosen. Different cuts and materials will invite different ways of moving. For example, if something is very loose, it might encourage a wobbly kind of walk, and if something is very tight-fitting it could lead to precise walk.

- Recalling the colours work of Chapter 4, move in response to any of the colours in the clothes that you have ended up with. Yellow might make you move with a lightness, red with some aggression and blue with a ponderous quality. Let the colour somehow dictate to you.

- If you have big clash of colours, that may create a sense of contradiction in your walk, going fast but not sure where you are going, for instance.

- The patterns on the clothes might suggest something to you. A checked pattern on the clothes could lead to a choppy kind of walking pattern, and stripes might well lead to an ordered, more elegant walk.

With all of the stages of these exercises, make sure that you are open to feeling the funny side of them. The work is meant to be light-hearted. Be on the look-out for what could be described as an internal laugh or smile. Whether you are playing a comic character, a fool or even a tragic character, you are always in play. You will discover, as the chapter goes on, the clown and *bouffon* exercises lead to two main explorations. One is of the clownish characters in Shakespeare, and the other is of creativity and play itself. This dressing up exercise, beyond encouraging a sense of 'freedom' (Lecoq, 2000: 156) and fun, may also have a practical application in the rehearsal room. As an actor in a Lecoq-inspired ensemble, you are likely to have taken some responsibility for costuming yourself and this exercise may inspire certain ideas or choices. You will want to have costume available in the rehearsal room from the earliest possible time, so that costume, movement and character grow organically within the process of discovery of the play itself.

Showing it off

- Get everyone to stand in a circle and see what people have come up with. Bizarre combinations, ill-fitting things and disastrous fashion faux-pas are useful.

- Everyone, in turn, should do a little spin on the spot to show off their outfit.

- Encourage the group to offer praise for some of the most unusual or unlikely items and combinations. It is a game.

- Once you have all spun around once, go around the circle again but this time each performer has thirty seconds to show off something further about the costume they have concocted. This should be done using movement and sound but no words. It may be a way of lifting a hat, clicking shoes or stroking the fabric.

- Each actor now splits off to explore on their own, anything that amuses them about the outfit they have assembled: the swish of a skirt, the anonymity of dark glasses or the surprise of a brightly coloured lining to a jacket.

- Allow the exploration in movement to veer towards a dance, or ritual. In a fuller clown pedagogy, students are encouraged to seek out a signature walk, or way of being as a clown. It is enough for us here to recommend a way of moving that feels fun and relatively uninhibited for the purposes of rehearsing with abandon.

- Add sound to the exploration. Shakespeare's characters will speak at some point, and the exploration of abstract or simply unintelligent sound at this juncture will help to develop the 'poetic matrix' of your character. What they look like, sound like and act like is under the stewardship of the actor as well as designer and director.

Connecting to Shakespeare

Often the actor's primary concern when playing a Shakespeare character is to connect to the emotional and psychological aspects of it. As you may have already realized, in this book, we often take you down an abstract road to reach a theatrical reality for play, be it with animals, colours or levels of tension. Now, in the realm of the *clownesque*, we will lead you into ever more seemingly silly ways to release Shakespeare's texts.

- Assemble a costume in the way we have described.
- Choose a speech to work on, comic or not.
- For the purposes of this exercise, imagine that you are guided principally by the costume choices.
- Find at least three things to do which relate directly to the costume as in lifting a hat, clicking shoes or stroking the fabric.

These little details become part of what a comedian might call '*shtick*' – a Yiddish word for comic business. You play around with them for a bit, expanding on whatever feels funny to you. This kind of approach is particularly useful for approaching Shakespeare's clowns. One such is the Porter in *Macbeth*. He appears soon after the high drama of King Duncan's murder and serves as pressure release for the audience before the tension multiplies as the murder is discovered. It is traditionally seen as a place for an actor (or clown) to extemporize, as for instance, Steven Noonan did in the RSC's 1999 production, ad libbing with references to the then prime minister Tony Blair.

Here is an example of what the costume game meeting the Porter's speech might be like.

First, develop your *schtick* from the costume, for instance:

1. Something wildly out of fashion and ill-fitting gives you the opportunity to strut somewhat as if it were marvellous.

2. You have a hat with an elastic under the chin; it can therefore be raised up with one hand and let go to slap or ping back onto your head.

3. You have a swishy skirt which makes you feel young and in love as you swirl it from side to side in a flirtatious way.

- Now work on the speech while foregrounding the comic *schtick* you have created from the costume. This means putting your physical (which could also become vocal) games first before any consideration of psychology or narrative.

    PORTER

    1) Here's a knocking indeed: if a man were porter of Hell Gate, he should have old turning the key. (*Knock*).

    2) Knock, knock, knock. Who's there, i'th' name of Belzebub? Here's a farmer that hanged himself on th'expectation of plenty. Come in time.
    1) Have napkins enow about you; here you'll sweat for't. (*Knock*)
    2) Knock, knock. Who's there, in th'other devil's name?
    3) Faith, here's an equivocator that could swear in both the scales against either scale, who committed treason enough for God's sake, yet could not equivocate to heaven. O, come in, equivocator. (*Knock*)
    2) Knock, knock, knock. Who's there?
    3) Faith, here's an English tailor come hither, for stealing out of a French hose.
    1) Come in, tailor; here you may roast your goose. (*Knock*)
    2) Knock, knock. Never at quiet. What are you?

1) But this place is too cold for hell. I'll
devil-porter it no further.
3) I had thought to have let in some of all professions
that go the primrose way to the everlasting bonfire.
   (*Knock*)
2) Anon, anon, I pray you, remember the porter.

(Mac. 2.3.1-20)

So in our example you might incorporate your (1) strutting as the
porter presents themselves to the audience as a ridiculous person
and then when you hear the knocking it creates a Pavlovian
response of (2) lifting the hat and letting it ping back; a kind of 'hell'
of repeated self-inflicted harm, and potentially very funny and (3)
the swishing of your skirt, creates a kind of whimsical meandering
into conjuring the different people you imagine at the gate: the
'farmer' and the 'equivocator'. We have indicated in the text where
you would activate your *schtick*.

- Once you have pushed yourself to the extremes of being
  driven by the costume-created *schtick* only, then you can free
  things up, keep whatever feels useful or move onto another
  way into the speech.

- At a more radical level you could take your silly costume
  games and apply them in the most serious of situations, for
  instance, for Lady Macbeth when she invokes the spirit of
  manliness to take her over to find the strength to kill:

LADY MACBETH
1) The raven himself is hoarse
That croaks the fatal entrance of Duncan
Under my battlements.
                     2) Come you spirits
That tend on mortal thoughts, unsex me here,
And fill me from the crown to the toe, top-full
Of direst cruelty.
                     2a) Make thick my blood,
Stop up th'access and passage to remorse,
That no compunctious visitings of nature
Shake my fell purpose, nor keep peace between

Th'effect and it. Come to my woman's breasts,
And take my milk for gall, you murdering ministers,
Wherever, in your sightless substances,
You wait on nature's mischief.
                              1) Come thick night,
And pall thee in the dunnest smoke of hell,
That my keen knife see not the wound it makes,
Nor heaven peep through the blanket of the dark
To cry, 'Hold, hold'.
Enter Macbeth.
                              3) Great Glamis, worthy Cawdor,
Greater than both, by the all-hail hereafter,
Thy letters have transported me beyond
This ignorant present, and I feel now
The future in the instant.

(*Mac.* 1.5.38-58)

- Imagine therefore that you are limited, as with the Porter's speech, to the *shtick* you have found in your clothing-based routine. It will mean that, to start with, you strut, ping your hat and swish your skirt to feed this speech. The strutting (1) could be sustained through the first few lines to give you a feeling of pumped-up awkwardness as the idea starts to form. You ping your hat (2) as you summon 'spirits'; the pinging of your head with hat unsexes you from 'the crown to the toe top-full'. The pinging of the hat might become more vicious as (2a) you start to allow more violence into your imaginings. You go back to the awkward strut for (1) 'Come thick night' as if, once again, the mystery of it all is bewildering in its extreme violence, only to move onto a girlish swishing of your skirt (3) when your unsuspecting husband and potential murderer arrives, 'Great Glamis' to 'in the instant'.
- It seems madness, almost, to approach it in this way, but the beauty of it is that you will be drawn so far away from the usual clichés of Lady Macbeth if you try something this radical, that space will open up in your actor's mind-body to make it work, and what seems comic to start with becomes, possibly, more terrifying and exciting because you are not delving into to stock activities and tropes of a much

played character. As ever, even if you come out with just one brilliant idea or gesture that feels genuinely correct and vivid for your portrayal then the clownish exercise will have done its job.

Putting a routine together

Previously, you have put together a small routine based on clothing. You can create a routine without it necessarily being based on clothes. We will now lead you towards another routine with which to explore a funny speech and a serious one. As with so many of the strategies laid out in the book, the way to discovering interesting and useful influences on the work is to improvise and play. To prepare for this we suggest that you follow the following steps from an adaptation of a John Wright game (Wright, 2006: 32).

Finding a game

- Spread out in the space. On a signal from the leader, you all make a gesture. It can be anything but don't make it complicated. In fact, the simpler the better.
- Once you have made a gesture or even just a small movement, like turning your head, lifting your toes off the floor, or poking your elbow out to the side, then start to play with it. This could be anything that takes your fancy. Simply repeating it is a kind of play. You may then vary it a bit. It can go faster, slower or take up more or less space. You might pretend you don't want others to see you doing it or try to outdo yourself each time you attempt it.
- Before long you will get bored and need to allow it to turn into something else. Turning your head might turn into flicking your head in both directions like a double take. The lifting of the toes might become the start of a jigging of your whole body and the poking of the elbow might turn into pretending to nudge someone.
- These games can be quite abstract or feel like they are more like acting.

- Try the same thing at least four times so that you start from just a tiny gesture each time and spend about a minute exploring, expanding and letting each of them mutate into whatever feels fun or even funny to you.

- After several minutes of exploration in movement and sound, encourage everyone to create some sort of simple routine of four different things which have come out of the play session. This can be very simple. Here is a template which might be useful:

  1. An entrance: a way of coming into the space that feels fun
  2. A way of moving through the space
  3. Some kind of flourish
  4. An ending or way of going off.

- It needs to be presentational. It is not acting. It is a performance.

Let us give you an example. You

1. enter giggling,
2. move around the space with great authority,
3. perform a kung-fu style kick in the air,
4. move off, flapping part of your clothing like a bird's wings.

It will feel silly and you may feel quite exposed. At an early part of the process of creating a comic character, you, the actor, must feel free to be silly, yourself and just a little crazy.

You can watch a simple version of this routine using Video 7: https://bloomsbury.pub/shakespeare-and-lecoq

Connecting to Shakespeare

As we do several times in this chapter, we are going to encourage you to explore a comic character with a routine that you have created and then use the same routine to explore a serious moment. Of course, when you work on this on your own, you will find your own routine and, additionally, you can, of course, expand on your routine, depending on time and enthusiasm. We have provided the bare minimum earlier as a guide and we will continue to use this for simplicity's sake.

Let us take the Nurse's speech from *Romeo and Juliet* where she talks of Juliet when she was a baby:

NURSE
Even or odd of all days in the year,
Come Lammas Eve at night shall she be fourteen.
Susan and she, God rest all Christian souls,
Were of an age. Well, Susan is with God;
She was too good for me. But as I said,
On Lammas Eve at night shall she be fourteen,
That shall she, marry! I remember it well.

(RJ, 1.3.17-23)

According to our previous example (**giggling**, **authority**, **kung-fu** and **flapping**) you would now combine the two – the speech and the routine. You allow the routine to take precedence over the characterization, psychology or emotion to start with. We will offer up a few lines as an example:

- (**giggle**) 'Even or odd'.
- (**walk with authority**) 'of all days in the year, / Come Lammas Eve at night shall she be'
- (**kung-fu kick**) 'fourteen'.
- (**flapping clothes like wings**) 'Susan and she, God rest all Christian souls, / Were of an age. Well, Susan is with God;'
- (**giggle**). 'She was too good for me'.
- and so on.

On paper, it looks schematic, but we are giving you a blueprint, as a way of bringing a sense of freedom and anarchy that the clown creates. Also, the combination of the routine with the Nurse's speech has been somewhat randomly created, but if you look carefully, you will notice that (1) the giggle with 'Even or odd' could suggest a nervousness on the Nurse's part, (2) the authoritative walk on, 'of all days in the year, / Come Lammas Eve, at night she shall be' might suggest her collecting herself, and (3) the kung-fu kick on 'fourteen' might release a moment of triumph at Juliet's progress through life.

The next two things, flapping and giggling, again, might harness, respectively, the Nurse's way of dealing with the loss of her daughter and the pleasure at her story that is to follow. As you read it you may not think it is necessarily appropriate but you will recognize, we hope, that it creates a kind of freedom and playfulness.

Now we will take a serious speech from the beginning of *A Midsummer Night's Dream* where Egeus comes to Theseus, the Duke, to complain about his daughter, Hermia's, behaviour:

> EGEUS
> Full of vexation come I, with complaint
> Against my child, my daughter Hermia.
> Stand forth, Demetrius. My noble lord,
> This man hath my consent to marry her.
> Stand forth, Lysander. And my gracious duke,
> This man hath bewitched the bosom of my child.
> Thou, thou, Lysander, thou hast given her rhymes
> And interchanged love-tokens with my child;
> Thou hast, by moonlight, at her window sung,
> With faining voice, verses of feigning love,
> And stolen the impression of her fantasy;
> With bracelets of thy hair, rings, gauds, conceits,
> Knacks, trifles, nosegays, sweetmeats (messengers
> Of strong prevailment in unhardened youth),
> With cunning hast thou filched my daughter's heart,
>
> (*MND*, 1.1.22-36)

As you look at the speech and think about our routine of **giggling**, **flapping** and so on, it could create a sense of cognitive dissonance. It will no doubt seem wildly inappropriate. One of the main aims of this chapter is to let clowning and *bouffon* lead you, and the ensemble, into a liberated space where anything, at least to start with, is allowed.

Try the following bit of dialogue with the clownish routine grafted onto it:

- (**giggle**) 'Full of vexation come I, with complaint / Against my child, my daughter Hermia. / Stand forth, Demetrius. My noble lord, / This man hath my consent to marry her.'
- (**walk with authority**) 'Stand forth, Lysander. And my gracious duke, / This man hath bewitched the bosom of my'

- (kung-fu kick) 'child'
- (flapping clothes like wings) 'Thou, thou, Lysander, thou hast given her rhymes, / And interchanged love-tokens with my child';
- And so on.

Although these choices may seem willfully odd, there is great value in seeing how the routine finds a way of making some sense in relation to the speech. The **giggle** may be a sign of Egeus having been pushed over his limit of rationality; the **authoritative** walk, a calling himself to order; the **kung-fu** kick an outburst of violent emotion and the **flapping** of wing-like clothes, an expression of some kind of disgust or even sublimated envy at Lysander's ability to create poetry. As ever, on Lecoq's lead, you should think about taking the movements involved to the maximum and then reducing them down to make them manifest as an internal sensation.

The *bouffon*

In this section we will introduce you to some of the areas that link Lecoq's *bouffons* to Shakespeare's fools. The fool and the *bouffon* are almost interchangeable terms. Indeed, David Bradby, in his translation of *The Moving Body,* explaining his retention of the French word *'bouffon'*, rather than the use of the English word 'buffoon' asserts: 'The French word suggests a grotesque comic while retaining overtones of medieval mummers and licensed court fools such as the one who accompanies King Lear in Shakespeare's tragedy' (2000: xxxix).

In *The Moving Body,* Lecoq writes:

No one is more of a child than the bouffon and no one is more of a bouffon than a child. This is why, in parallel with the work on the body, we do preparatory improvisations leading towards the bouffonesque dimension on the theme of 'Childhood'. We try to find our way back to childhood using different techniques. (2000: 132)

The clown and the *bouffon,* or fool, are linked very strongly by play. 'Play', as we have explored, is a central tenet of Lecoq's pedagogy.

The *bouffon* is the area in the training where play runs riot. The first step to accessing the *bouffon* is to play at being children. The Shakespearean fool is also playful. His intent may be didactic – to teach his employer something about themselves, often by mocking them, as Lear's Fool mocks or teases the King (*KL*) or Feste mocks Olivia (*TN*) for her extended mourning. However, fools are able to mock (and thereby teach) because they are seen, in some ways, to be only playing, and this state of play keeps them immune from punishment. They talk in riddles and rhymes, as children enjoy doing.

In *The Moving Body,* Lecoq also explains that *bouffons* are 'people who believe in nothing and make fun of everything' (2000: 124). He explains that as his *bouffons* evolved, 'many variations' developed, the first being 'parody' – 'making fun of another person by means of mimicry' (2000: 124). This is the second facet of the *bouffon* that we will explore in this chapter.

These *bouffon* exercises are not only useful for actors playing 'fool' characters. Any of the following exercises can be used for preparing for a fool or for any other character, and indeed, as we will explore, many of Shakespeare's characters have childlike or childish elements to them.

Pretending to be children

Lecoq asserts, 'In Italy they go on stage and play. That is my idea too' (2000: 71). Play is to children what work is to adults. Children are the experts in play and so for much of the rest of this chapter, we will be encouraging you to take their lead and let the child-state appear.

Lecoq-influenced companies are prone to allow the games that they play to bleed into their productions. In Footsbarn's productions, the games often swamp the play altogether. As Dominic Dromgoole, former artistic director of Shakespeare's Globe, said of the company: 'They are wild and imaginative. It's liberating, particularly for British audiences, to see Shakespeare done this way. They bugger about with it' (Gardner, 2008). Complicité are more respectful of the texts than Footsbarn but still work very playfully. They played the children's game, Blindman's Buff, in rehearsal for their production of *The Winter's Tale,* finding that this particular game gave the ensemble an evocative way in to staging Act 2, Scene

1 in which Mamilius is playing with his mother and her ladies (Arden: 2022).

Playground

- Gather your ensemble together and clear as much space as you can.

- Invite the group to enact being in a playground as children between the ages of four and eight.

- It will likely be chaotic and fun for some and mildly distressing for others.

- After a few minutes, stop and discuss. Notice the kind of energy you have exhibited in your attempt to recall your childhood.

- Take some time now to think back to how you might have been at this age. There will be, of course, many aspects of a complex childhood you may wish to include or not include. Stay with what you feel comfortable exposing. This will change and develop the more you and your group grow together and trust one another. Repeat the playground exercise before moving on.

Some 'children' will latch on to others. Some will suggest games and others will be happy to follow. Some will sulk for a while, and others will look for fights or trouble. Children form gangs and clubs and all sorts of hierarchies. There is a huge amount of fun and interest to be had in this area if you want to pursue it. We will make a start in the following few exercises.

The children organize a game

This next exercise is an *auto-cours*, and at the Lecoq school it gets prepared over several hours. You can do it more as a mini-*auto-cours*. Give yourselves half an hour to work on it before you share it with the company.

- Split into small groups of four or five. In this *auto-cours* you are going to be a version of the child that you were between the age of four and eight.

- As a group of children, improvise the organizing of a game such as Chase, Hide and Seek, It, Grandmother's Footsteps or even some game that no one has ever heard of.
- Make sure that one person stays out of each group to oversee what happens.
- Improvise on the theme of organizing a game for around five minutes.
- After about five minutes bring the improvisation to a halt and discuss, briefly, how it has gone, as your adult selves.
- Improvise again on the same theme of children organizing a game for five minutes.
- Stop and discuss what you have done, but as the children you are playing. It may not be a very constructive conversation and is, in some ways, a continuation of the improvisation itself, but it will shed more light on the kind of child that each of you is channelling.

There is plenty of potential for play here, as the arguments and negotiations between the 'children' are as important, if not more important, as playing the game itself. The strategy of discussing the improvisation in character creates a grey area and it blurs the lines between make-believe and reality, acting and not-acting. This is the area that *bouffon* and the fool live in.

- Improvise the same theme again, having an ever-clearer picture for yourselves of how the power dynamics work within the group of 'children'.
- After five minutes, stop and discuss one more time, as your adult selves, how you might make something of what you have improvised .
- Devise the above into a short showing for the rest of the group. The theme is **children organizing a game**. It should last no more than two or three minutes.
- Each group takes turns to present the work to the others.

This work is quite demanding but is very good for getting closer to the spirit of the *bouffon* and the fool. The children that appear will have their own particular slant on the organizing and playing of a game. Some may be bossy, some hugely enthusiastic, some shy, some wild, others highly imaginative and some very literal. The basic pattern you fall into will help to form the basis of your fooling and will also help to release spontaneity in any character.

Connecting to Shakespeare

- Take any scene you are working on and allow the work on children to inform it. This can be done in a number of ways. Here are a few examples:

a. Allow the actors, as children, to organize the rehearsal of the scene itself. This will create a kind of anarchic meta-narrative which will, in turn, create an interesting energy for the eventual version of the scene.

b. Play the actual written scene with the actors pushing their interpretation of the childlike qualities that they feel are possible within the character that they are playing. So, if for example an actor is playing Hamlet in the first encounter with the court in 1.2, they may well allow themselves fully into sulk, pout and tantrum modes. The actor playing Claudius, on the other hand, may indulge in much childish grandstanding, relishing openly the sway they have over others.

c. Work on the state of childhood may also influence a production to fully embody particular characters as children, for example Ariel in *The Tempest*, Puck in *A Midsummer Night's Dream* and the witches in *Macbeth*, all who have been portrayed on stage as or by children.

The childhood sequence

To help clarify what is most useful to you from your investigation into childhood you will now create a childhood sequence.

- Spend about fifteen minutes exploring, alone, some of the things that emerge for you about being a child between the ages of four and eight. You will need to act these things out. You are, in effect, being the child you once were, in various guises.

- Look for variety of mood and activity. Think of different situations. At home, at school, with friends, on your own, in private, at meals, at bedtime, excited, bored, complaining, explaining, tantrumming, somewhere new, somewhere familiar.
- Play at things which have some movement in them. Use sound and words if you like, but use words sparingly as you will need most of what you do to be in movement.
- Choose five varied things, for example:

    1. Skipping to school
    2. Arguing with your best friend
    3. Dreaming of flying
    4. Drawing doodles with great precision
    5. Playing with a pet.

- Make a sequence out of them. This is the same, in essence, as the sequence for **lugubrious** or any of the Passion Pots in Chapter 7 in that you will need to improvise in movement to develop it. It is more involved, however, and will take longer to create.
- After fifteen minutes or so, put all the five things together in a sequence. Put them in an order that pleases you. At this stage allow your activities to be relatively realistic.

Depending on the time you have, show each of the childhood sequences to the group at this stage. Apart from anything, it is a very good ensemble-building activity. But if you are more pressed for time, go on to the next stage straightway.

- Rework and refine what you have done so far, making it more focused. Allow the movements to become a little more abstracted and a bit more in the direction of being choreographed.
- As you rework it, allow yourself to include abstracted sound and/or words in what you do.
- Find a way of doing the whole thing in just ninety seconds. Show it to the company. Watch as many of them as you can. See how each of them has a unique world to it. This world, the rhythmical life and the dynamic range of each of these

little showings could form something of the back-bone to your *bouffon* and any of Shakespeare's fools that you play.

- Find a way of doing it all in just a minute. Show again.
- You now have a condensed childhood sequence.

Connecting the childhood sequence to a fool

We will not be creating a *bouffon* with you here, in the same way as we do not have the scope to take you fully into clowning in this book but you will use your childhood sequence in a similar way to how you deployed the discoveries in the four elements as discussed in Chapter 6.

Let's take a speech from a fool as an example. It is Touchstone from *As You Like It*. Touchstone, along with Rosalind, has just witnessed the shepherd, Silvius, declaiming about his unrequited love for the shepherdess Phoebe. When Rosalind comments: 'Alas, poor shepherd, searching of thy wound / I have by hard adventure found mine own', he responds:

TOUCHSTONE
And I mine. I remember when I was in
love I broke my sword upon a stone and bid him take
that for coming a-night to Jane Smile; and I remember
the kissing of her batlet , and the cow's dugs that her
pretty chopped hands had milked; and I remember the
wooing of a peascod instead of her, from whom I took
two cods, and, giving her them again, said with weeping
tears: 'Wear these for my sake.' We that are true lovers
run into strange capers. But as all is mortal in nature, so
is all nature in love mortal in folly.

(AYL, 2.4.43-52)

We will take a twin-pronged approach to this – first, working solo and, second, working with a partner who claps and calls out the stages of the sequence.

Working solo

- Go through the whole speech in each of the stages of your childhood sequence. This means working on the speech five times, each time colouring it heavily with one of the childhood aspects that you have found. In our case:

1. Skipping to school
2. You are arguing with your best friend
3. Dreaming of flying
4. Drawing carefully
5. Playing with your pet.

- Once you have explored the speech once in each of the five aspects of childhood, you can progress to a more nuanced exploration, using whichever parts of the sequence feel most useful for the speech in hand.

Working in a pair

- Go through the speech, but this time ask somebody to clap at random moments during the speech and call out a different part of your childhood sequence.

This is a very valuable exercise in creating flexibility. One of the beautiful qualities that we can learn or re-learn from children is how completely they can invest themselves in the moment and also how quickly they can change tack if something else takes their interest.

The *bouffon* (or childhood sequence in this book) brings unpredictability to bear on any situation. By their unpredictability the *bouffon* challenges the status quo or what is perceived to be normal. Rosalind comments back to Touchstone as soon as he has uttered the abovementioned lines, that, 'Thou speak'st wiser than thou art ware of' (2.4.53). This, of course, is the whole point. The fool or *bouffon* obfuscates to make more sense and deviates to reveal to others the truths about themselves.

Connecting the childhood sequence to a non-fool character

- Imagine now that you are playing Rosalind and you have the childhood sequence from above: (1) **skipping,** (2) **arguing,**

(3) **dreaming**, (4) **doodling** and (5) **petting**. In the following
speech, Rosalind is berating the shepherdess Phoebe, for the
way she treats the young man who loves her, called Silvius.
Rosalind is, at this time, pretending to be a boy called
Ganymede:

ROSALIND
[*Advances.*]
And why, I pray you? Who might be your mother,
That you insult, exult, and all at once
Over the wretched? What though you have no beauty –
As by my faith I see no more in you
Than without candle may go dark to bed –
Must you be therefore proud and pitiless?
Why, what means this? Why do you look on me?
I see no more in you than in the ordinary
Of Nature's sale-work. 'Od's my little life,
I think she means to tangle my eyes too!
No, faith, proud mistress, hope not after it.
'Tis not your inky brows, your black silk hair,
Your bugle eyeballs, nor your cheek of cream,
That can entame my spirits to your worship.
                                    (*AYL*, 3.5.36-49)

- In the same way, as with Touchstone, play the speech in each
  of the modes 1–5 from the childhood sequence. Exaggerate
  the movement and any sound that you have found for each
  of the childhood sequence aspects as you do it.
- Now repeat the speech in each phase of the childhood
  sequence. But this time reduce and contain the movement in
  order to feel how the sequence motivates you more subtly.
- Do another version where you ask a colleague to clap and
  shout out various different parts of the sequence to you as
  you do the speech and you have to adapt what you are doing
  to their command.
- Having got to know the speech in this way, now free it up so
  that you use whatever part of the sequence feels useful.

As you explore from mode to mode, whether big or small, declared
or subtly nuanced, you are learning the words in a deeper way and

also training yourself to not fix how you are going to do the speech. As with all of our suggestions, we are putting you into an exploratory mode so that you feel creative and flexible when it comes to rehearsing the scenes. There is much to be said for allowing the child part of you loose on the characters and stories in Shakespeare. The child-aspect is educated out of people as they grow and socialize into society, but it is very useful to find the kind of jealous rage of Leontes (*WT*), the caprice of Olivia (*TN*), the dreaminess of Richard II, or the braggadocio of Falstaff. Most of our favourite characters in the plays stick out to us because they are lacking a piece of the maturity that would render them as more effective social animals but not as dramatic characters. And for the Shakespeare's fools, their job is to play as children might and to reflect back to their masters and to the audience the truth that a child might stumble upon without knowing that they have done so.

Mockery

As Lecoq says in *The Moving Body*, the *bouffon* is a creature who 'believes in nothing and makes fun of everything' (2000: 124). It is a pretty extreme state of mind. In order to at least touch on that state in this book we are going to turn to an exercise from Lecoq himself (actually a clown exercise in his pedagogical journey but one which serves well here as a build-up to *bouffon* too) involving copying the way others in the group walk and then exaggerating it for comic effect.

Copying and exaggerating

- Find some space. Divide yourselves into pairs and elect yourselves to be A and B.

- All the A's walk around the space. Try to walk normally. Walk as you feel you probably do when you are not conscious of being watched. It is not obvious. B is watching very carefully. This need only last a minute or so.

- B now walks around the space copying, as closely as possible what A did. Did they lean forward a bit, tilt to the side or hang back somewhat? Did one arm move more than the other? Did they look about or stare straight ahead. B's job is to try and show how A walks. This stage of the exercise often results in much laughter as the recognition of your ingrained patterns creates a slightly febrile atmosphere.

- Now B rests while A copies what B did. So, A is doing a copy of a copy of their own walk. It is a kind of *transposition*. In effect, you are exaggerating your own walk.

- As you walk in this way, try to find the pleasure in the exaggeration and go as far as leaning into anything you feel is funny about it. See how natural you can make the walk even though you are exaggerating by feeling that even though you are becoming larger than life that it feels truthful to you in some way.

- Make sure that both A and B get to the stage of copying a copy of their own walk, and feeling the joy in exaggerating themselves.

Connecting to Shakespeare by copying your character

The first stage of making fun or mocking is to exaggerate. It is good to be able to start with yourself before you start making fun of others. Having read the play text a few times and when you feel you have an idea of roughly what your character is like then try the following:

- Take a few moments to imagine your character walking. You may want to do this with your eyes closed or open but the key is to imagine them as being distinct from your body. It is like A watching B above, but now B is your character rather than another person in the group.
- Copy the walk that you see in your mind's eye.
- Exaggerate the walk you have just done.
- Exaggerate the walk wildly.

Imagine you are playing Emilia in *Othello*.

- You see her walking around the space in your mind's eye.
- You copy this walk as faithfully as you can. Notice how that makes you feel. It may give you sensations of efficiency, brightness and watchfulness.

- Now exaggerate this walk. You will find yourself changing from your own habitual walk and almost magically disappearing into someone else's skin.

- Find whatever pleasure you can in this. Even though this is not a comic part, find what feels funny about it to you. It doesn't mean you will be playing her as comedy but being aware of any oddity, tick, or particularity in her may well help to specify her for you and the audience, and it may help to humanize her too.

- Exaggerate wildly the walk and all that you have discovered up to now. This will feel over-the-top and even grotesque.

- Find sound for this walk and maybe a tune. You are entering into the *bouffonesque* now. She becomes almost ritualized. Your grotesque version of Emilia acts as a way of making fun of her. It is not just a spoof of Emilia though. If you connect and commit clearly to the exaggeration, which may well now feel more abstract than realistic, you may be touching on some of the issues buried in the part and the play. The pain of being married to Iago, the subservience required of figures like Emilia and Desdemona and her fierce, almost poetic nature might surface somehow in movement and sound.

- As ever with these explorations, see if you can take whatever you are doing to the extreme. Explore Emilia as if she was a creature from another planet but with some of her essential characteristics intact. Once you have done this, you are free then to compress whatever you have done to suit your preferences and the needs of the production.

- Try to do the same as above but with the whole company, either improvising around scenes or playing them as they are written but with varying degrees of exaggeration of their characters.

A trait in Lecoq-informed productions of Shakespeare is how the physicality of characters will often be exaggerated, taking the character beyond the individual into what you might call the archetypal space. Philippe Hottier in Mnouschinke's 1982 Théâtre du Soleil production of *Twelfth Night* made an extraordinary impression by playing Sir Toby so bent over by a life of drinking that he is catapulted off-course by his own mis-managed balance as part of his way of walking and being. Daniel Chrisostomou, in Flabbergast's 2022 *Macbeth,* transformed mesmerizingly into a broken, gnarled King Duncan, pushing the reality of an old man into the realms of the totemic and the late great Marcello Magni's locomotion for his Autolycus in Complicité's 1992 *The Winter's Tale* was hardly walking at all, but fizzing with an almost combustible lurch from trick to trick played on those around him. This ability to exaggerate gleefully is not just to make fun of or just to find grotesques, but on a more modest level to find size. Shakespeare's characters, by virtue of the colour and complexity with which they were originally imagined by the author and with the centuries of accrued reputation can take and require great boldness to unite their individuality and archetypal qualities. This exaggeration could also be what Lecoq called 'essentialization'. It is what Simon McBurney calls 'le geste en-dessous' ('the gesture underneath') (McBurney, 2022). It is a way of driving at the heart of the theatrical essence of a moment, or character or scene. The great Shakespearean director Peter Brook is quoted in John Heilpern's *Conference of the Birds,* as warning actors against acting with sincerity: '"Be insincere", he tells them with a smile'. (1977: 179). Reverence for Shakespeare's great texts can lead us to fight shy of their true theatrical potential, so this exercise in exaggerating is helpful in making sure that at some point you blow the crust of received wisdom off the play and find, even with the dynamite of mockery, something that is essential to the play but is also vital to your group's need to put the play on.

9

Exploring staging

Shakespeare's plays can, of course, be staged in myriad ways. In the last twenty years there have been experiments with playing in 'shared light' at the reconstructed Shakespeare's Globe Theatre in London; table-top versions by Forced Entertainment, staged with cruets, sauce bottles and glassware standing in for characters; versions performed on pop-up trestles by the Handlebards using only the objects and costumes the four actors can carry on bicycles; and Gregory Gudgeon's extraordinary, one-man, puppet-filled, audience-participation *Richard II*, to name but a few. The reason that many theatre-makers come back to Shakespeare is that the plays have 'a vast imaginative space' (Alexander, 2022) and it is the play of space that we will dwell on for our last chapter.

First, we will offer up a version of one of Lecoq's most well-known and adaptable exercises, which involves balancing the stage by means of an imaginary plate on a fulcrum. We will encourage you to see and feel space anew with some exercises derived from what is known as *le LEM*. Alongside the two-year training at Lecoq, there has been another optional course, which has used Lecoq's extensive study of architectural space which he conducted alongside Krikor Belekian. We will share with you a couple of exercises using sticks, part of the *LEM* toolkit, to encourage what Briony O'Callaghan calls the 'masked space' (O'Callaghan, 2022) and what Aurelian Koch, a master of the architectural side of Lecoq's training, calls 'experiential space' (Koch, 2022). We will then explore the movement of the chorus in relation to materials.

Choruses are not native to the Shakespearean landscape but are often used in productions and in some ways the whole company can be seen to operate as a chorus. Moving on from here, we will introduce a strategy, based on Ariane Mnouchkine's radical out-front playing style.

Balancing the stage

Le Plateau

This exercise, a form of which is written out in *The Moving Body* (2020: 141–4), explores what Mnouchkine describes as 'some of the essential rules of staging' (Morris, 2016: 154). Shona Morris explains that it has a long association with Shakespeare and the staging of his work, through the legacy of Michel Saint-Denis:

> At an event celebrating Michel Saint-Denis' legacy run by Struan Leslie at the Royal Shakespeare Company (RSC), Mark Evans led a session on Lecoq's Plateau. Clifford Rose recalled how The Plateau had been taught by Michel Saint-Denis when he ran classes for the RSC Studio 13 in the 1960s. (2016: 154)

Simple version

We will begin with a simple version of the exercise, drawing on Lecoq's account. We will then proceed, as Lecoq does, to a version of the exercise that divides the ensemble into a hero and chorus. Finally, we will suggest that the hero/chorus exercise can be extended into one in which there are two opposing groups, balancing each other, while retaining an internal balance. There are lessons to be learnt from each of these exercises in terms of staging a range of scenes from Shakespeare's plays.

Lecoq's version of the exercise begins with a 'rectangular stage', surrounded by benches, which, the actor is asked to imagine, is 'balanced around a central axis' (Lecoq, 2020: 142). Whether or not you have benches, you will need to mark out a rectangle, either with chairs or with tape. This should be as large a space as you can manage.

- The company should assemble around the edges of the rectangle, spread as evenly as possible. They may sit, or ideally, stand, since this creates a greater sense of readiness.
- One actor (A) places themselves in the centre of the space – creating a sense of balance. You might want to imagine that the stage is a rectangular platter balancing on a stick, or, as Christian Darley suggests in her book, *The Space to Move*, a raft 'balanced precariously on the point of a cone' (2009: 131) or floating on the sea.
- Actor A begins, according to Lecoq, to 'warm up' the centre of the *plateau* 'so as to bring it to life' (2000: 142). What this means, in practice, is that actor A should take some time to take in the 'audience' on four sides and to experiment with a sense of balancing on the mid-point. They might tease the audience with the potential of tipping up the *plateau*.
- At a certain point A will chose to move away from the centre. At this point another actor has to step in and balance the imaginary platter. This can be anyone who is standing or sitting around the outside, but it should only be one person. If more than one person attempts to rescue the situation, then someone must give way. This actor is now 'B'.
- Actor B now has responsibility for moving the game on. They should move around the stage, while A responds in order to keep the *plateau* balanced.
- There are a few points to note as the game progresses:

    a. The size of individual actors is irrelevant. For the purposes of this version of the game we imagine that everyone has an equal 'weight'.

    b. This is a game. It should have an element of tension and a sense of fun.

    c. You should play the game slowly to begin with. It is also helpful to start out thinking that you are in Levels three to four of tension (see Chapter 4, pp. 75–6) – reasonably calm with a keen sense of anticipation. You

> will need to allow the group some time to grasp the
> principals of moving and balancing.
>
> d. At the point at which a new actor enters the stage,
>   there should be a moment of suspension.
>
> e. Don't feel the need to rush. It is an investigation of
>   balance, power and space and not a drama in itself.

- At a certain point A decides to NOT respond to B so that the space is no longer balanced and another actor (who will become 'C') must enter to balance the space once more.

- After a moment of suspension, C takes the lead. C will move to where they want, and in whatever rhythm they choose. A and B have to respond together to keep the balance until such time as one or both of them choose not to respond or to disrupt the sense of balance. A fourth actor (D) will enter the game.

- This continues for as long as you can sustain it. Usually, it gets muddled above about five people on the *plateau*. It may take some time to get the hang of the exercise. You may also notice, as Lecoq did, that actors tend towards easily recognisable shapes and formations: 'When there are three of them, they tend to form an equilateral triangle; four a square, five a circle'. Lecoq described such formations as lacking dynamism – 'these positions . . . do not make for a playable dramatic situation' (2000: 143). You should aim to find irregular, interesting formations that still create balance.

This is one of the key learning outcomes of this simple version of the exercise – to see what shapes and formations create drama and interest.

Learning to balance a stage is essential for any Shakespeare production. This exercise is a great way to encourage a company to realize that staging can be organic, provided that actors respond with intelligence and sensitivity to one another. Whether you are dealing with scenes involving only two characters or those involving fifteen or more, there is a need to make sure that the space is continually in and out of balance to create interest. As Catherine Alexander, who uses this exercise regularly in teaching Shakespeare, says, 'It is about power and space' (Alexander, 2022).

Finding variations with the plateau

Once you have been through the version of the previous exercise a few times, you may start to bring in variations.

- When you are leading try out various actions to see how they alter the balancing of the space. Here are some suggestions.

  1. When you find a new position on the plateau, crouch down and see how it affects what the other players feel they need to do.
  2. When you are leading, make yourself bigger by spreading your arms. Does it make you 'heavier' or 'lighter'?
  3. Try lying down and see what the other players need to do to keep the stage balanced.
  4. As leader, jump up and down. Spin. Try looking at the others in a friendly way. Or be stern. Notice that the way you are dictates to a degree how the stage must re-balance itself.

As Lecoq says, it requires 'experimentation' (2000: 142). The players on the outside are as crucial as those on the *plateau* itself. Do not feel like you are looking for 'storytelling performance on a realist stage, but to experience the sensations of fullness and emptiness'. The point is to develop a 'shared sense of being present in the space' (Lecoq, 2000: 143).

Once you have got really sharp at knowing when to join in and how to balance the space with a degree of finesse, you can move on to exploring Shakespeare's scenes with this tool. Shakespeare abounds with heavily populated scenes and this exercise is a perfect way to get an embodied insight into how to stage them with actors having an enhanced sensitivity to one another and the spatial dynamics of power.

Connecting to Shakespeare

Before attempting a scene under *plateau* conditions, let the actors explore characters without scene or narrative but just their presence and how they move.

- Start again with the actors around the edge of the rectangle but this time they are in character.
- Notice which character wants to come to the centre. How do they warm it up? How long before they move off?
- Do certain characters avoid one another and other stick together?

There is so much scenic freedom in Shakespeare's plays that this exercise will give you an organic insight into how the characters negotiate space under their own steam.

Connecting to Shakespeare's text

There are a number of ways of employing the *plateau* in the preparation of staging a scene. Think about using it at various stages of its development. You can explore a scene with this method before you have rehearsed it, while you rehearse it and when you have nearly perfected it. Here is where a director or teacher can come in very useful as they will be responsible for setting up various rules for the game to work well.

We are going to provide an example of how to apply the basic *plateau* exercise to 2.1 of *A Midsummer Night's Dream*. In the text, a fairy enters from one side and Puck from the other. They are alone for a time before Titania and Oberon enter. Do this with text, with book in hand if necessary.

- Play the game with the fairy and Puck first. Try it in two different ways:

  1. Make it so that the actor speaking is leading the movement and the other has to balance the space.
  2. Make it so that the one who is listening leads.

Just with those investigations you will motivate the actors to make interesting staging suggestions. You are not yet staging the play but empowering the actors to make felt decisions about how to unbalance and re-balance the space which will give you great ideas going forward into a more formal staging session.

- Bring the actors playing Oberon and Titania into the game. Try a couple of minutes of script each time with these various rules:

1. First, suggest that Titania is leading and everyone must balance the plateau around her.
2. Next do the same with Oberon and see how different things are.
3. See what happens if everyone balances the space around Puck.
4. As is natural in the scene, let Oberon and Puck form a pair and Titania team up with The Fairy. The two pairs play the game of balancing the space.

As in the original game, it is an experiment, and so the most useful thing is to be vigilant about how the balancing of the space works and how it does not work. This game adds a liveness to the staging. The actors' awareness of each other's physical presence takes you beyond the limits of just talking at one another. When you come to put the scene onstage, among other things, you will find that the balancing can be very useful in encouraging the actors to find space apart from each other when the scene becomes intense. So often actors get close when in high stakes and this exercise will encourage them to keep exploring the stage and create space between them even when it is getting tense. It will also help actors to not stand in lines, which is often the death of any scene.

Hero and chorus

We now move to Lecoq's second iteration of the exercise, simplified slightly for the sake of ease. The exercise begins in the same way, with A in the centre. A is the 'hero' (Lecoq, 2000: 144).

- At a moment of their choosing, B enters the space. They play the game of unbalancing and balancing the *plateau.*
- At a certain point, C chooses to enter the space. This is the point at which the game changes. C does not balance the space equally with A and B. Instead, they join B, to become the 'chorus'. The chorus is of equal weight to the hero and must balance the space accordingly. So A = B + C.
- Now, each time another actor enters the space, they join the chorus and continue to balance A, who remains the leader.

This exercise can be useful for thinking about scenes where there is a protagonist and a crowd. The protagonist is 'in charge' of the space, and the crowd must balance out the space in relation to him. Remember, that, as with the simple version of the exercise, you should try to avoid geometrical formations and find interest in the shapes created.

Connecting to Shakespeare – Applying the *Plateau* to highly populated scenes

One of the most useful things about the chorus version of the game above is to notice and play with how the chorus moves and how it makes its collective decisions. It takes time to let this develop. Before you try all this out on your own play, here is a brief mention of a scene in which individuals must balance the space, then small groups and then larger ones.

It is 1.1. in *Romeo and Juliet*. The first scene where the warring households spar and fight.

- The scene begins with Sampson and Gregory (both Capulets) onstage, balancing the space.

- These men of the house of Capulet are joined by two of the Montagues, and now the two groups need to balance the stage.

- As the scene continues they are joined by Benvolio (Montague), Tybalt (Capulet), Citizens (either side), Old Capulet and Lady Capulet, Old Montague and Lady Montague.

- As each character or group of characters come on, make sure that the first thing that happens is that the new arrival becomes the leader and the rest of the characters have to balance the stage in response to whatever they do.

- Once characters are in groups they must feel how to balance themselves within their group as well as in relation to the leading character.

There are many ways to explore and develop a robust sense of how characters, stretch, manipulate and react to each other in this staging exercise. Lecoq-trained teacher Sabina Netherclift says of the *Plateau* that it 'demands that actors have absolute clarity as to

why they are moving and how they will affect others in the scene'
(Netherclift, 2022).

Shaping the space of the play

There are three references to Shakespeare in *The Moving Body*. One
is to *The Tempest* in relation to *The Fundamental Journey* (Lecoq,
2000: 42); the second, a passing mention to the use of Shakespeare's
texts, along with those of Molière, Goldoni, Goethe and others
in the second year of training (2000: 123) and this one, from the
section about the *LEM*, which is run alongside the main training,
and specializes in exploring, in more depth, how humans and space
interact. Lecoq is musing on what the *LEM* is not:

> Taking *Hamlet* as a theme would obviously not involve learning
> how to construct the set for the first act, but rather showing
> the future scenographer how spaces must be constructed which
> *await* the drama to be played out. When he inscribes in the space
> the scenography of *Hamlet*, the space itself will hold the density
> of the drama. He will have understood that performances are not
> given in front of a set, but in a dynamic construction where the
> actors can play with the space.
>
> (2000: 166)

What, in brief, Lecoq is saying, is that his aim was to encourage
designers not to build what he called a 'monument' (Koch, 2022)
as a set for actors to move in front of, but to inculcate into his
protégés the need to keep exploring how space might be used and
changed as an organic human process during the making of a show.
An example of this is how Complicité hold off on design decisions,
even in major subsidized theatres, until the design formulates itself
through the play of the actors in rehearsal.

The *LEM* processes are too specialized to go into in this book,
but we would like to share with you a paired back version of them,
in the first of these stick exercises, courtesy of Aurelian Koch, who
studied under Lecoq, formed a company, Bouge-de-là, and now
teaches under the banner of Spacelab. In his own words, he is 'no
Shakespearean', but his insights and exercises can be bent towards
Shakespeare with relative ease (Koch, 2022).

Manipulating a stick

At various points in the book we have encouraged you to hold back from assigning meaning too early. We are now going to give you some exercises that help to transfer the full responsibility for creating a design for a production, from the designer to the ensemble, as we encourage the actors to explore and animate the space.

You will need a stick, ideally, for everyone in the company. Bamboo sticks from the garden centre are best. Complicité are pretty precise in their education pack about the sticks, stating that they should be '6 foot' and 'very straight' (Complicité, n.d).

- Ask an actor to come into the space with a stick. The company form a kind of audience, placed however you want: in front, on three sides and so on. In a similar way to the clown and *bouffon* exercises, simply allow the actor to 'play' with the stick and see what they do with it.

- There are some predictable outcomes here. Often an actor will want to make the stick into something else, a guitar, or a rifle or broom. Let them do so.

- Once they have done that, ask if there is anything else that can become of the stick. Another popular choice is to use it percussively, to tap or bang it.

- At this point, ask if the actor can just let the stick be a stick, or not even a stick but a long line to which they are attached and which is in space. This will be a challenge. The point is to de-familiarize the stick.

- Encourage the actor to simply move the stick, more as if it were a puppet. They can hold it horizontally, and make it go up and down, or create curved movements, or any kind of improvised motion which seems to suggest something beyond the actor or the stick.

- Notice how different movements of the stick seem to suggest different spaces, and how the connection between the stick and the space might even suggest a feeling or atmosphere. For instance, is if the stick goes, horizontally, very slowly, up in front of the actor then a vast space opens up, and if the stick is swizzled to the side then an amusing space of possibilities could be created. This is almost impossible to explain, and as Koch himself said 'you have to experience it to understand it' (Koch, 2022).

Connecting to Shakespeare monologues

- Ask one actor to consider a speech from a play but only with the stick used in the 'puppeted' way we have just described.
- Let's take a tragic speech from *Othello*. Othello is contemplating murdering his wife:

> OTHELLO
> It is the cause, it is the cause, my soul!
> Let me not name it to you, you chaste stars,
> It is the cause. Yet I'll not shed her blood
> Nor scar that whiter skin of hers than snow
> And smooth as monumental alabaster:
> Yet she must die, else she'll betray more men.
> Put out the light, and then put out the light!
> If I quench thee, thou flaming minister,
> I can again thy former light restore
> Should I repent me. But once put out thy light,
> Thou cunning'st pattern of excelling nature,
> I know not where is that Promethean heat
> That can thy light relume: when I have plucked the rose
> I cannot give it vital growth again,
> It needs must wither.
>
> (*Othello*. 5.2.1-15)

- Have an actor, who is not playing Othello, read the speech while the actor who is playing the part improvises in the space with a stick.
- The actor must be relieved of all responsibility to do well, or make it make sense. It has to be a gut reaction to the words and sounds that are being uttered.
- Ask the actor with the stick to hold it mostly with two hands and to keep some distance between them and it. It is not a 'prop'. It is simply a vessel for the actor's spatial response to the speech.

- Ask the actor reading to go quite slowly and ask the actor with the stick to not feel the need to describe or animate everything they hear but to make broad and relatively slow motions with the stick as if they were actually carving, illuminating and creating the space around them.

- Repeat the exercise a couple of times, to allow the actor with the stick a chance to change their mind about things and for the company to see new spaces open up.

- Allow the stick to go into one hand sometimes but be wary of it becoming a tool or weapon.

- Now allow the actor playing Othello to have a go at speaking the speech while continuing to improvise with the stick.

The stick forces bold and articulate choices from the actor. The speech suddenly becomes, via the actor's movement, not just a private discourse between his inner world and the body of his wife but a publicly shared artistic expression. The speech transposes itself into a moveable sculpture of spatial scenography. The stick in space will automatically bring us to the potential of the public nature of the poetic utterance. This is one route to a poetic dimension of the 'masked space' (O'Callaghan, 2022).

Group stick improvisations in spatial scenography

In the opening scene of *Hamlet*, the text suggests that the characters are on the ramparts of the castle. It is dark. There seems to be a tense and suspicious atmosphere. If you start with a blank canvas with no decisions made about how to play the scene or what the set will be like, you can employ the sticks as a group to explore some possibilities of 'experiential space' (Koch, 2022).

Enter **Barnardo** *and* **Francisco**, *two sentinels.*
BARNARDO
Who's there?

FRANCISCO
Nay, answer me. Stand and unfold yourself.

BARNARDO
Long live the King.

FRANCISCO
                         Barnardo?

BARNARDO
                                          He.

FRANCISCO
You come most carefully upon your hour.

BARNARDO
'Tis now struck twelve. Get thee to bed, Francisco.
                                          (*Ham.* 1.1.1-5)

- Five actors have sticks and will move, in a kind of chorus, with 'puppeted' sticks as collective response to whatever they hear in the lines from the play which will be read out. It is improvised and so is as much about connecting the actors to an embodied, kinetic, appreciation of spatial possibilities in the scene as anything else.

- This is an improvisation and it can be done many times until something interesting and useful shows up. The ensemble will need to have a feel for one another, and be well-versed in listening to one another.

- Have somebody read out one line at a time and ask all five actors to find something to do with their stick which feels appropriate to the atmosphere, meaning, dynamics of the line spoken.

- As each line is read out, the chorus of five should find a way of carrying, moving and articulating the stick that feels interesting in terms of the whole abstract picture.

- You should aim to work together to create an abstract realization of the space of the scene.

- Try to do this with minimal discussion, though the less experienced you are of working together the more you may have to negotiate in the initial stages.

Here are some suggestions for what might emerge:

1. 'Who's there?'

    Sticks swirl slowly and suddenly stop.

2. 'Nay answer me. Stand, and unfold yourself.'

    Sticks charge across the space and are then lifted up.

3. 'Long live the King.'

    Most of the sticks move uniformly across the space with one wavering slightly.

4. 'Barnardo?'

    The sticks squirm a little and prod the space in front of them. One stick slowly uprights itself.

5. 'He.'

    The sticks form in tight bunches and move slowly away from one another.

6. 'You come most carefully upon your hour.'

    The sticks from one side soar up into the air, and the other group swim across the space close to the floor.

7. ''Tis now struck twelve. Get thee to bed, Francisco.'

    The sticks form a geometric shape and surge forward together before retreating upstage.

The idea here is to improvise freely but collectively with the sticks. Actors will tend to respond to the rhythm, sound and meaning of the lines. As you will tell from what we have written, some of the stick moves seem to make sense and some not so much sense. They are both equally important, at this stage of exploration. Declan Donnellan says about the early stages of rehearsing Shakespeare that you keep trying to get rid of meaning and 'the meaning will only get you so far; the body gets you further. You can come back to meaning but every word needs to be reborn through the body' (2021). The manipulating of space in this way can have multiple benefits from troubleshooting, to devising, to orchestrating the way in which, as Lecoq says, the actors are not going to just act in front of a set 'but in a dynamic construction where the actors can play with the space' (2000: 166).

The chorus

As discussed in the Introduction, the influence of ancient Greek drama and the chorus are present in the work of both Shakespeare and Lecoq. Although Shakespeare does not use a chorus in the way the Greeks did, there is still much to be gained from exploring Lecoq's techniques of embodied choruses for your work on Shakespeare, and many Lecoq-inspired companies include chorus work in their productions. In Cheek by Jowl's *Measure for Measure* (2013), the chorus was intended to be the embodiment of the psychology of Vincentio, the Duke; The National Theatre's *Othello* (2022) deployed a 'miming' chorus to 'represent inner demons' (Akbar, 2022) and Flabbergast's *Macbeth* (2022–3), working with Lecoq principles, framed the whole production with a collective of wild-eyed, mud-caked, drumming story-tellers, who also created a choric speaking moment which we will examine later.

Using materials for the chorus

As Lecoq says in *Theatre of Movement and Gesture*, 'the chorus is like a body – if it lacks a strong sense of mime then it loses its poetic qualities' (2006: 109) and in the Lecoq tradition, mime does not mean mime illusion of the sort that we might recognize from the street mime conjuring a wall or box that they are stuck in, it is more what we have described previously as *mimage*, a kind of recreating of phenomena through movement. The phenomenon we are going to visit next is often just referred to as 'materials'. Here is Lecoq on materials in relation to the neutral mask part of the journey:

> After the natural elements, work on identifications moves to different materials: wood, paper, cardboard, metal, liquids. For the actor, the objective is both to broaden his field of reference and to sense all the fine shades of difference which separate one material from another or which coexist within the same material. Substances which are doughy, unctuous, creamy, oily, all possess different dynamics. My aim is for the students to acquire a taste for such qualities, exactly as a gourmet will recognise the subtle differences between flavours. (2000: 45)

Phyllida Lloyd talks of 'avoiding psychology' in the rehearsal room. Declan Donnellan, working with his company Cheek by Jowl, asks actors to refrain from thinking about the precise meaning of the lines for as long as possible. One way to help actors to work in this way is to alert them to materials and how they move. A chorus or company might be inspired by the materiality of the four elements, or indeed by materials themselves, as for instance, in English Shakespeare Company's 1997 production of *A Midsummer Night's Dream,* which was propelled by the imaginative use of Sellotape and baskets. Lecoq's teaching invites the bodies of the actors to take on the properties of the materials themselves, thereby achieving theatrical *transposition* and spatial poetry. The next exercise is a wonderful example.

Sugar lump

You will need a glass with water and a sugar lump for this exercise.

- Assemble your actors and have them watch what happens when a sugar lump is put into a glass of water.
- Immediately afterwards, attempt to re-enact this as precisely as possible.

You will notice first bubbles rising up from the sugar lump, and then there is a wait. The sugar lump will dissolve, but slowly. You will start to see granules falling off, and an increasing sense of collapse. As this progresses, you will notice some parts of the sugar remaining upright, and stranded, like ruins or pillars. Eventually the whole edifice of the sugar lump will subside and collapse on the bottom of the glass.

- Actors will need to be particularly attentive to others as the group organically figures out, without any instruction, how best to collectively re-enact the drama in the glass.

It has a kind of tragic quality, where the inevitability of the collapse is seemingly fought off by the pillars of sugar which stand for a while. GH Zonana, who teaches this exercise at the Oxford School of Drama, tells of how powerful it was being taught this exercise at the Lecoq school by Paola Rizza, who remarked of the improvising group that was slowly disintegrating, that 'all civilisations end like this; in ruins' (GH Zonana, 2023) It is a great example of how Lecoq's teaching stretches the minds of its students, from the accessibly mundane to the audaciously poetic, dramatic and philosophical.

Connecting to Shakespeare

- Find a moment in the play which involves one or two protagonists and a group. It could be, for instance, speakers and a crowd in a Roman play, a king and his courtiers in a history play, or families and friends in tragedies or comedies to whom someone delivers news.
- First, ask a group or chorus re-enact the sugar lump collapse as accurately as possible, but with the moment from the play in question at the back of their minds.

- Now run the part of the play you have chosen and find the right moment for the group or chorus to start its bubbling, disintegration and slow decline.

- Embrace the fact that the materiality of the sugar disintegration will pull the scene out of shape for a while, but what can be learnt, and witnessed, by the embodiment of the phenomenon will repay you handsomely in terms of throwing up staging ideas that, when mixed with Shakespeare's language, will potentially move the audience.

- Divide the group into two – one with those who address the crowd or assembled company (this may only be one person) and the other with the crowd or 'chorus' in attendance.

- The speaker(s) will be under the influence of the dissolving sugar lump as it disintegrates (slowly slipping away to the ground). The listeners will enact the opening moment of the sequence where the bubbles rise upwards (transposing this into their movement, breath or gaze).

- Once versions have been done with the pure movement of the sugar lump incorporated, you are free to do with it whatever seems most appropriate to your production.

Here are a couple of moments from Shakespeare to inspire you to try this sugar lump exercise. You could also try the exercise with any number of alternative materials, from a crumpled plastic bag (or better still, a cellophane wrapper) slowly and irregularly opening up, to two groups or individuals as cardboard, being ripped unevenly in two.

Richard II 3.2

In this scene from *Richard II*, Richard and his followers have landed in Wales. Richard discourses on death and kingship.

- Imagine those who are listening to Richard under the influence of the melting sugar lump.

KING RICHARD
No matter where. Of comfort no man speak!
Let's talk of graves, of worms and epitaphs,
Make dust our paper and with rainy eyes
Write sorrow on the bosom of the earth.
Let's choose executors and talk of wills.
And yet not so, for what can we bequeath
Save our deposed bodies to the ground?
Our lands, our lives and all are Bolingbroke's,
And nothing can we call our own but death
And that small model of the barren earth
Which serves as paste and cover to our bones.
For God's sake let us sit upon the ground
And tell sad stories of the death of kings –

(R2, 3.2.144-156)

- Then reverse it so that you imagine Richard's courtiers holding their positions, while the actor playing Richard collapses slowly as the sugar melts.

Romeo and Juliet (5.3)

In this final scene, Friar Laurence describes, to the assembled company, including Lord and Lady Capulet, and Lord Montague, the events that led up to the death of Romeo and Juliet.

- Imagine that, in an attempt to go beyond psychology and tap into a deeper resource of theatrical staging, the Capulets and Montague are 'motored' (Lecoq, 2000: 41) by the movement of the dissolving sugar cube. Parents, under the pressure of extreme grief are unpredictable, and liable to behave irrationally. This simple technique of taking the stage movement beyond the grasp of psychology, in following the material collapse, is likely to release the actors, beyond their rational thoughts, to allow them to enter, physically, the horror of the moment.

FRIAR LAURENCE
I will be brief, for my short date of breath
Is not so long as is a tedious tale.
Romeo, there dead, was husband to that Juliet,
And she, there dead, that's Romeo's faithful wife.
I married them, and their stol'n marriage day
Was Tybalt's doomsday, whose untimely death
Banished the new-made bridegroom from this city;
For whom, and not for Tybalt, Juliet pined.
You, to remove that siege of grief from her,
Betrothed and would have married her perforce
To County Paris. Then comes she to me,
And with wild looks bid me devise some mean
To rid her from this second marriage,
Or in my cell there would she kill herself.

(RJ, 5.3.229-242)

- Now reverse this and see what it is like with the actor portraying Friar Laurence, imitating the dissolving sugar as they deliver this speech.

Depending on the play on which you are working, you might want to observe and embody other materials – elastic, shattered glass, oil.

Speaking as a chorus

> To speak through another's mouth, in a common choral voice, is to be, at one and the same time, grounded in the truth of a living character, and in touch with a dimension which transcends human reality. (Lecoq, 2000: 135)

Henry Maynard, whose Flabbergast Theatre, influenced by Lecoq, produced a viscerally dynamic production of *Macbeth* (2021), explains how they decided to use a chorus to speak the Captain's description of Macbeth's heroism in Act 1, Scene 2 – 'Doubtful it stood [. . .] upon our battlements'.

> Part of it was ensemble building and we wanted to tell the audience that it was an ensemble show and that we are interested in European theatre art, and it's not going to be a version of the play in army fatigues with a bloke with a bit of blood on his face. We felt that it would have a really nice impact at the early stage of the play and a chance to include some choreography, and to try to tell the story. (Maynard, 2022)

In the production this speech is taken on by various members of the ensemble, moving it from an individual's account into a staged story-telling episode.

As Maiya Murphy details:

> While the Greek chorus is typically approached as a group of performers speaking together, a Lecoquian investigation starts with choral work as a group of performers moving together. The Greek tragic language will become an extension of that movement . . . When the time comes to address language, it is addressed 'through the body'. (Murphy, 2018: 175)

Once again, Lecoq's description of this process in *The Moving Body* is somewhat elusive:

> The tragic chorus speaks with a single voice and the group of actors has to be able to achieve this collective dimension. For ensemble speaking, different techniques are used: one student recites a text that all have learned, another tries to speak the same text through the mouth of the first; gradually others join in until they achieve a common group voice, each member of the group having the impression that he is spoken by the others. This group voice is often moving and extremely beautiful. (2000: 150)

We suggest that in order to achieve the 'collective dimension' of 'ensemble speaking', actors need to begin by learning to breathe together and make sound together, before finally speaking as a group.

These initial exercises are about sensing when to do something together as a group.

Breathing together

- Ask the group to stand in a circle facing inwards.
- The members of the group need to be very attentive to one another, which will mean listening and sensing each other's rhythms and breathing.
- The group is going to attempt to take a deep breath, all at the same time, without anyone obviously leading.
- Allow the group to take their time over this.
- You will need to do it a few times before you achieve this 'ensemble' breath.
- Now the group should come together in a triangle formation, so they are no longer facing each other, but are close enough to be able to sense one another's breathing and impulses.
- Repeat the 'ensemble' breath in the new formation.
- You can try all of the variations of this exercise in different stage formations – whatever seems most appropriate to your production and to the number of chorus members.

Humming together

- Remain in whatever formation you have settled on.
- Now the group is going to add some sound to the breath.
- Using the same process as above, this time the group will need to breathe in together and vocalize the outbreath on a hum, beginning the hum at the same time.
- Ideally the sound that the group creates together will be a pleasant one. Again, some practice will be needed to achieve this.
- The group is going to repeat the previous exercise, with the breathing and vocalizing on a hum, but this time the group should aim to come off the hum at the same time.

Humming and vocalizing together

- In this third variation the group begins by breathing in together and humming together.

- Once the group has achieved the hum, they will all try to open out the sound to an 'Ah' at the same time and then come off the 'Ah' as a group.

Speaking together

- For this variation of the exercise, you will need to take the first few lines of the Captain's speech:

  > Doubtful it stood
  > As two spent swimmers, that do cling together,
  > And choke their art. The merciless Macdonald
  > (Worthy to be a rebel, for to that
  > The multiplying villainies of nature
  > Do swarm upon him) from the Western Isles
  > Of kerns and galloglasses is supplied,
  > And Fortune, on his damned quarry smiling,
  > Showed like a rebel's whore. (Mac. 1.2.7-15)

- Using the same process as mentioned earlier, the group is going to attempt to breathe in together, and then speak the word 'Doubtful' as a chorus.

- It may take a few goes to achieve this. Once you have done so, you should attempt to speak the whole line together.

- You can, continue with this exercise until you have built up to multiple lines – with the chorus speaking in unison throughout.

Sharing a chorus speech

It is likely, when presenting a speech as a chorus, that you will want to speak some lines in unison and some individually. This exercise helps the chorus to explore ways of sharing a chorus speech between speakers, passing the lines instinctively from one to another.

- Begin by walking around the space trying to keep an even distance from one another.

- One person has an imaginary ball.
- That person should make eye contact with another, as you move around, and 'throw' them the imaginary ball.
- The person who receives the 'ball' should receive the energy and intention of the thrower, before passing the 'ball' on to someone else.
- The whole group will have to remain attentive so that the ball can be passed without hesitation.
- Once you have mastered this exercise with the imaginary ball you are going to 'throw' the lines of the speech to one another.
- Start moving through the space again.
- One person begins, with the line 'Doubtful it stood . . .'
- At whatever point in the speech they choose (after three words or three lines) they 'throw' the speech to another speaker.
- The important thing to remember is to receive the energy and intention of the previous speaker and then transform it into your own energy and intention as you speak.
- The second speaker then 'throws' the speech to a third and so on, until the whole speech has been spoken.
- Once the group has got used to 'throwing' lines to one another, repeat the exercise, moving around the space, but instead of actively 'throwing' a line to another actor, you will simply pass the line by making eye contact.
- This will involve a great deal of concentration.
- Try to keep the notion of picking up the energy and intention of the previous speaker.
- Pass the lines in this way until you have spoken the whole speech.

When it comes to incorporating this work into your production, you may choose to combine these exercises, with some lines delivered in unison and some by individuals. You will probably choose, eventually, to decide on who is speaking which line, but even if you do this, try to keep the sense of passing or throwing lines to one another, and keeping the momentum of the speech going.

Facing the audience

Shakespeare's theatre was fundamentally an outdoor theatre like the Greek tragedy, medieval mystery plays and Commedia Dell'Arte that preceded it. Peter Hall says of the difference between nineteenth- and twentieth-century naturalism and early modern drama that, 'In this indoor experience, we overhear the action and are disturbed by it. In the outdoor day-lit experience, we are challenged by it as if it was a public meeting' (2000: 62). There is much in the Lecoq training which leans towards the 'public meeting' as opposed to the overheard theatre of the darkened room.

Darren Tunstall writes:

> as a result of the kind of shared imaginative work that Lecoq elicited from the actor, the actor becomes more attuned to the audience. This, to my mind, is one of the great gifts of Lecoq's pedagogy for any artist seeking to bring to the public a renewed and invigorated sense of Shakespeare's value. Lecoq taught us how to listen to – in a sense, how to think like – the audience. (2016: 273)

One of the key themes that reoccur when considering the ways in which the pedagogy of Lecoq can be deployed for a Shakespeare production is how the training incorporates a consideration of the audience or *le public* as fundamental. Students are not encouraged to delve consciously into their own emotions or indulge themselves in any way. The audience leads. Most theatre-makers will claim to hold their audience in high esteem, and yet there is something synergistic between the low-tech performance space of Lecoq's *grand salle* and the early modern shared-light space of The Globe Theatre that Shakespeare mainly wrote for.

The highly sophisticated productions of Mnouchkine, in the 1980s, were all played with the actors almost entirely delivering the text directly out to the audience. In interview, she is quoted as saying that the fourth wall is not only unsuitable for Shakespeare but 'deadly'. She explains: 'In rehearsal every time the actors found them-selves talking *to each other*, it didn't work. I said to them, "Tell it to the audience". It's the secret one must never lose' (Williams, 1998: 94). She admits in the same interview that it is 'extremely difficult to do' and in a comment which relates helpfully to the last exercise in Chapter 7, she clarifies that, 'When the "state", the passion that [the actor] must express in relation to the character, is not sufficiently clear, there's always a tendency to take refuge in a psychological relationship with one's partner on-stage' (David Williams, 1998: 94).

- Choose a piece of dialogue from your play.

If you would like to try the exercise straight away then use this dialogue from *2 Henry IV*. It is an easy-going conversation between two old friends.

SHALLOW. Come on, come on, come on: give me your hand, sir, give me your hand, sir; an early stirrer, by the rood! And how doth my good cousin Silence?

SILENCE. Good morrow, good cousin Shallow.

SHALLOW. And how doth my cousin your bedfellow? and your fairest daughter and mine, my god-daughter Ellen?

SILENCE. Alas, a black woosel , cousin Shallow!

SHALLOW. By yea and no , sir: I dare say my cousin William is become a good scholar; he is at Oxford still, is he not?

SILENCE. Indeed, sir, to my cost.

SHALLOW. A must then to the Inns o' Court shortly: I was once of Clement's Inn, where I think they will talk of mad Shallow yet.

SILENCE. You were called 'lusty Shallow' then, cousin.

SHALLOW. By the mass, I was called anything, and I would have done anything indeed too, and roundly too.

(*2H4*, 3.2.1-17)

- Play the scene facing each other.
- Then play the scene with both actors facing directly out into what will be the audience space.

In our example, the text explicitly suggests that Silence and Shallow shake hands which mitigates against playing out, but still stick to the exercise and you will notice how the attempt to fulfil both requirements will induce extra creativity.

- Notice the differences and discuss the benefits and disadvantages of both versions.
- In the spirit of opening this out to the audience, make another series of attempts to play the dialogue out, rather than to each other, with some of our suggestions as to how to think about the relationship between the out-front space and the other actor.

  1. Treat the lines you deliver to the audience as something that they will, in turn, give to your playing partner. A series of gifts. Imagine your outstretched arms as you deliver the gift, and the outstretched arms of the audience as they 'give' the line back to your playing partner.

  2. Think of each line, or section of text, however you feel like dividing it up, as challenges to the audience. Imagine launching your lines with some kind of apparatus, a tennis racket, a medieval sling or trumpet sound. Imagine that the audience will continue, whatever method you have used, to transmit the lines to your playing partner.

  3. Try treating each of your lines as a hilarious joke which you have heard and which you tell to the audience and expect them to pass on to your playing partner.

- Go over what you have done and see how much of the scene you can make work, playing it as out-front as possible. You may not feel as bold as to fulfil Mnouchkine's suggestion of playing the whole scene facing forwards, but you will definitely get a strong impression of how the balance between what is communicated via the audience and what is delivered directly between the actors could be shifted in favour of out-front. Put another way, have you done enough to make it feel possible to deliver lines to your playing partner but via the audience as a 'fixed point of reference' (Tunstall, 2016: 271).

It should be added here that Soleil's extraordinary productions, which toured the world to great acclaim, are very stylized and unlike much you are likely to see in the contemporary Shakespearean landscape, but we are delving into their work here with regularity as we believe, that with so many Lecoq-trained company members and a director who is so aligned in so many ways with Lecoq's ethos, although their productions were demanding, they truly represented a rare theatrical *transposition*.

Lecoq says in *The Moving Body*,

> a theatre school should not always journey in the wake of existing theatre forms. On the contrary, it should have a visionary aspect, developing new languages of the stage and thus assisting in the renewal of theatre itself. This is what we have achieved with our rediscovery of masks, the chorus, clowns, *bouffons*, etc., all of which have enriched innumerable new performances. (Lecoq, 2000: 172)

Lecoq asked his students to find, through the laws of movement, the essence of things. Whether finding new ways to tell old stories, or embodying Shakespeare's full texts, what is essential will vary from place to place and era to era, but we hope that we have managed to show how closely aligned Shakespeare and Lecoq are in their wish to grapple, playfully and poetically with ways of portraying the human condition on the stage and that you have gained some insight into how you and your ensemble might treat the plays with a fresh and physical approach.

BIBLIOGRAPHY

Akbar, Arifa (2022), 'Review of Othello', *The Guardian*, 1 December.

Alexander, Catherine (2018), 'Theatre de Complicité and Story Telling'. Available online: https://www.bl.uk/20th-century-literature/articles/theatre-de-complicite-and-storytelling (accessed 1 March 2023).

Alexander, Catherine (2022), Interview with Ed Woodall, conducted on 22 December 2022.

Arden, Annabel (2021), Interview with Ed Woodall, conducted on 20 June 2021.

Arden, Annabel (2022), Interview with Ed Woodall, conducted on 4 July 2022.

Barton, John (1984), *Playing Shakespeare*, London: Methuen.

Bloom, Harold (1998), *Shakespeare: The Invention of the Human*, London: Fourth Estate.

Bradby, David (2000), 'Translator's Note', in Jacques Lecoq, *The Moving Body*, xxxix–xl, Reprint 2020, London: Methuen.

Britannica, Editors of Encyclopaedia (2021a, February 12), *Lupercalia. Encyclopedia Britannica*. https://www.britannica.com/topic/Lupercalia (accessed 1 March 2023).

Britannica, Editors of Encyclopaedia (2021b, December 16), *horned toad. Encyclopedia Britannica*. https://www.britannica.com/animal/horned -toad (accessed 1 March 2023).

Britton, John (2013), *Encountering Ensemble*, London: Bloomsbury.

Complicité, 'Teachers' Notes: Devising'. http://www.complicite.org/media /1439372000Complicite_Teachers_pack.pdf (accessed 1 March 2023).

Craik, Katherine A., ed. (2020), *Shakespeare and Emotion*, Cambridge: Cambridge University Press.

Crystal, David and Ben Crystal (2002), *Shakespeare's Words*, London: Penguin.

Darley, Christian (2009), *The Space to Move*, London: Nick Hern.

Dixon, Tom (2022), Interview with Ed Woodall, conducted on 2 December 2022.

Donnellan, Declan (2021), *Not True, But Useful: A Cheek by Jowl Podcast*. Series 4 episode 2. https://open.spotify.com/episode/2aX

rKPYL31jhYcA2pJlGUw?si=PHiUWNczSsaRfqriKdC5Ng (accessed 1 March 2023).

Ecole Lecoq (2020), 'LEM Program'. http://www.ecole-jacqueslecoq.com/lem-presentation/?lang=en; http://www.ecole-jacqueslecoq.com/lem-program/?lang=en (accessed 1 March 2023).

Escolme, Bridget (2013), *Emotional Excess on the Shakespearean Stage*, London: Bloomsbury.

Evans, Mark (2006), *Jacques Copeau*, Reprint 2018, London: Routledge.

Flabbergast (2010), 'About Flabbergast'. http://www.flabbergasttheatre.co.uk/about.html (accessed 1 March 2023).

Footsbarn Travelling Theatre (2023), 'About Us'. https://www.footsbarn.com/about-us/ (accessed 1 March 2023).

Fry, Michael (2015), 'Theatre de Complicité', in Graham Saunders (ed.), *British Theatre Companies 1980–1994*, 165–88, London: Bloomsbury.

Gardner, Lyn (2008), 'All the World's a Tightrope', *The Guardian*, 21 May.

Gilrain, Jennie (2016), 'The Mimo-dynamics of Music, Poetry, and Short Story: Lecoq on Bartók', in Mark Evans and Rick Kemp (eds), *The Routledge Companion to Jacques Lecoq*, 127–34, London: Routledge.

Godwin, Grace (2017), 'Basquiat Cases: Hamlet, Doctor Faustus, and The Alchemist at the Royal Shakespeare Company', *Shakespeare Bulletin* 35, no. 4: 675–86.

Gurr, Andrew (2004), *The Shakespeare Company 1594-1642*, Cambridge: Cambridge University Press.

Hall, Peter (2000), *Exposed by the Mask*, London: Oberon.

Hall, Peter (2003), *Shakespeare's Advice to the Players*, London: Oberon.

Heilpern, John (1977), *Conference of the Birds*, London: Faber.

Hoffman, Tiffany (2014), 'Coriolanus's Blush', in Evelyn B. Tribble, Lawrence Johnson, and John Sutton (eds), *Embodied Cognition and Shakespeare's Theatre: The Early Modern Body-Mind*, London: Routledge.

Hultquist, Aleksondra (2017), 'The Passions', in Susan Broomhall (ed.), *Early Modern Emotions: An Introduction*, 71–4, London: Routledge.

Jones, Toby (2022), Interview with Ed Woodall, conducted on 27 July 2022.

Knoepflmacher, U. C. (1963), 'The Humours as Symbolic Nucleus in Henry IV, Part 1', *College English* 24: 497–501.

Koch, Aurelian (2022), Interview with Ed Woodall, conducted on 30 November 2022.

Lecoq, Jacques (2000), *The Moving Body*, Reprint 2020, London: Methuen.

Lecoq, Jacques (2006), *Theatre of Movement and Gesture*, London: Routledge.

Les Deux Voyages de Jacques Lecoq (1998), (Film) Dir. Jean-Noël Roy and Jean-Gabriel Carasso, France: La Sept ARTE/ ANRAT/ On Line Productions.

Linklater, Kristin (1992), *Freeing Shakespeare's Voice*, New York: Theatre Communications Group.

Lloyd, Phyllida (2022), Interview with Ed Woodall, conducted on 24 October 2022.

Lust, Annette (2000), *From the Greek Mimes to Marcel Marceau and Beyond*, London: Scarecrow.

Mason, Bim (2016), 'Bouffons and the Grotesque', in Mark Evans and Rick Kemp (eds), *The Routledge Companion to Jacques Lecoq*, 157–64, London: Routledge.

Maynard, Henry (2022), Interview with Ed Woodall, conducted on 16 November 2022.

McBurney, Simon (2022), Interview with Ed Woodall, conducted on 5 December 2022.

Morris, Shona (2016), 'The Chorus', in Mark Evans and Rick Kemp (eds), *The Routledge Companion to Jacques Lecoq*, 150–8, London: Routledge.

McLeish, Kenneth and Stephen Unwin (1998), *A Pocket Guide to Shakespeare's Plays*, London: Faber.

Murphy, Maiya (2018), *Enacting Lecoq*, London: Palgrave Macmillan.

Murray, Simon (2018), *Jacques Lecoq*, London: Routledge.

Netherclift, Sabina (2022), Interview with Ed Woodall, conducted on 16 May 2022.

Noble, Adrian (2022), *How to Direct Shakespeare*, London: Bloomsbury.

Noble, Adrian (2009), *How to Do Shakespeare*, London: Routledge.

O'Callaghan, Briony (2022), Interview with Ed Woodall, conducted on 17 November 2022.

Paster, Gail Kern (2004), *Humouring the Body*, Chicago: University of Chicago Press.

Reid, Robert L. (1996–7), 'Humoral Psychology in Shakespeare's Henriad', *Comparative Drama* 30, no. 4: 471–502.

Peterson, Dave (2020), '"Thus, like the Formal Vice": Mark Rylance and Clowning in *Richard III*', *Comedy Studies* 11, no. 2: 239–52.

Preeshl, Artemis (2017), *Shakespeare and Commedia Dell'Arte: Play by Play*, London: Routledge.

Richardson, Helen (2016), 'Theatre du Soleil', in Mark Evans and Rick Kemp (eds), *The Routledge Companion to Jacques Lecoq*, 307–15, London: Routledge.

Richardson, Helen (2019), 'Ariane Mnouchkine', in Felicia Hardison (ed.), *The Great European Stage Directors*, vol. 7, 81–112, London: Methuen.

Roach, Joseph R. (1993), *The Player's Passion: Studies in the Science of Acting*, Ann Arbor: The University of Michigan Press.

Romersberger, Sara (2016), 'Lecoq's Clown and its Application to Playing Shakespeare's Clowns', in Mark Evans and Rick Kemp (eds), *The Routledge Companion to Jacques Lecoq*, 171–8, London: Routledge.

Rudlin, John (1994), *Commedia Dell'Arte: An Actor's Handbook*, London: Routledge.

Sachs, Claudia (2016), 'Bachelard, Jousse and Lecoq', in Mark Evans and Rick Kemp (eds), *The Routledge Companion to Jacques Lecoq*, 51–8, London: Routledge.

Shakespeare's Globe (2018), 'Globe Ensemble', https://www.shake spearesglobe.com/discover/globe-ensemble/ (accessed 2 March 2023).

Shannon, Laurie (2009), 'The Eight Animals of Shakespeare; Or, before the Human', *PMLA* 124, no. 2: 472–9.

Sher, Antony (1985), *Year of the King*, London: Methuen.

Sullivan, Erin (2015), 'Humours', in Michael Dobson, Stanley Well, Will Sharpe and Sullivan Erin (eds), *The Oxford Companion to Shakespeare*, 2nd edn, 822, Oxford: Oxford University Press.

Tashkiran, Ayse (2016), 'British Movement Directors', in Mark Evans and Rick Kemp (eds), *The Routledge Companion to Jacques Lecoq*, 227–35, London: Routledge.

Tashkiran, Ayse (2022), Interview with Ed Woodall, conducted on 7 December 2022.

Tunstall, Darren (2016), 'Lecoq and Shakespeare', in Mark Evans and Rick Kemp (eds), *The Routledge Companion to Jacques Lecoq*, 268–74, London: Routledge.

Valls-Russell, J. (2018), 'Footsbarn: Relocating Shakespeare in Molière's France', *Cahiers Élisabéthains* 96, no. 1: 117–30.

Williams, David (1998), *Collaborative Theatre: Le Theatre du Soleil*, London: Routledge.

Wright, John (2006), *Why Is That So Funny*, London: Nick Hern.

Zonana, GH (2023), Interview with Ed Woodall, conducted on 1 December 2022.

INDEX